GEE

The Diary of a National Hunt Jockey

GEE

The Diary of a National Hunt Jockey

Gee Armytage

Macdonald
Queen Anne Press

A *Queen Anne Press* BOOK

© Gee Armytage 1989

First published in Great Britain in 1989 by
Queen Anne Press, a division of
Macdonald & Co (Publishers) Ltd
66–73 Shoe Lane
London
EC4P 4AB

A member of Maxwell Pergamon Publishing Corporation plc

British Library Cataloguing in Publication Data
Armytage, Gee
  Gee – The Diary of a National Hunt Jockey
  1. National Hunt racing. Jockeys – Biographies
  I. Title
  798.4'5'0924

ISBN 0-356-17160-4

Typeset by Selectmove Ltd, London
Printed and bound in Great Britain by
Richard Clay Ltd, Bungay, Suffolk

To Mum and Dad,
who made everything possible

ACKNOWLEDGEMENTS

Besides the people mentioned in this book many others
have helped in 1988 and I hope many will continue to
help, lend advice and pick me up when I am down.

First, grateful thanks are due to Dad's generous owners
who consented to give me my first rides in public, particularly Gill Lawe, Nora Carroll and Susan Thomson;
those outside trainers for whom I rode my first winners,
Nigel Twiston-Davies, Ian Bell and John Spearing;
and of course Colin Tinkler, who gave me so many
opportunities, one of which resulted in my Cheltenham
win on The Ellier, and Geoff Hubbard and his assistant
Ferdie Murphy for being responsible for Gee-A among
several others.

Secondly, I must acknowledge those who have kept
a watchful eye on my career, in particular Stan Mellor,
Anthony Webber and Hywel Davies, not forgetting
Gordon Cramp and Andy O'Dwyer; and all who have
lessened the physical aches and pains after the heavier
falls, especially the doctor on my doorstep, Dr Baly,
and my long-suffering Aunt Linkie, whose skills as a
physiotherapist have been much appreciated.

Special thanks are also due to Richard Pitman for his
unstinting commitment to the cause of lady jockeys. It
would be unfair not to mention all my super friends for
their unfailing support, most of all Bism (Tina Cassan)
who, in my moments of depression in what has after all
not been a great year for me, was a tower of strength and
to whom I seem to have paid scant attention in my diary.

Gee Armytage
John Dorman, who helped Gee Armytage to write this
book, runs a writers' agency specialising in sports books,
and is also a director of a company which promotes
National Hunt racing overseas. He writes regular
racing features for *The Times* and the *Sporting Life*,
and assisted John Buckingham in writing his successful
autobiography, *Tales from the Weighing Room*. His most
recent project is a book about Desert Orchid. He lives in
Warwickshire.

Introduction

The life of a professional jump jockey is not always
the glamorous business it appears to be. The heady
moments of triumph in the winners' enclosure are far
outweighed by the daily grind of riding out, driving long
distances to the races, subjecting the body to a constant
near-starvation diet in order to make the minimum
weight. There is also the ever-present danger of being
thrown from a horse, or sustaining an injury which could
deprive a jockey of income for weeks, or worse than
that. In the period described in this book, one jockey
was killed on the racecourse and another was paralysed
for life.

For Gee Armytage, riding horses is in the blood. When
she was born in Oxford 23 years ago her father Roddy
was already training horses, and still does so. She has
lived all her life in the village of East Ilsley in Berkshire,
and competed in her first gymkhana at the age of three.
In her teens she was a successful showjumper, recording
two championship wins at Hickstead, and she took part
in her first race in public at the age of 16. Since then she
has won major races at the Cheltenham Festival meeting
and briefly led the 1988 Grand National on the horse with
which she is most closely associated, Gee-A.

In a profession which is still very much male-
dominated, where women riders are treated with contempt
by some of their male colleagues and as sex symbols by

the popular press, Gee Armytage, in 1988–89, her first season as a professional, has striven to prove that she can hold her own in competition with the best where it matters most – on the racecourse. This book is a record of how she went about it. It is not an out-and-out success story, but it does attempt to provide an inside view of a world where Gee, because of her sex, has to try that much harder than her male colleagues to achieve excellence.

Prologue
December 1987

1987 has been the most fantastic year for me. I started
it as a keen amateur scrounging for any ride I could get,
and I never expected half the luck and good fortune that
came my way. Teaming up with Mr Hubbard, England's
leading permit holder, and Gee-A, riding a double at the
Cheltenham Festival meeting and a winner at Aintree,
and retaining the lady jockeys' title with 18 winners were
all achievements I would never have predicted 12 months
ago.

This time last year, although I'd ridden the same
number of winners, I was well down on seven rivals for
the ladies' title, and I think this shows that in general
the women aren't doing so well this year. Of my main
rivals last season, Tarnya Nicholls is riding less often, and
Penny Ffitch-Heyes has problems with her collar-bone,
so at the moment I consider the principal contender to be
Diane Clay. She is well supported for rides by her father,
who is having a good season, and although she appears to
ride the bulk of her winners on the harder ground of the
early and late season, she is definitely someone to keep an
eye on.

It's not only the girls who are having a slow start this
season though: the amateurs are also suffering. I think
this is due to the new rule limiting them to only

75 rides a season. Any amateur who has much success and is offered plenty of good rides will be forced to turn professional now, and this is exactly what has happened to me. At the start of this season I had decided to remain amateur, partly because of the difficulties girls have progressing as professionals without an allowance, and partly because I desperately wanted to be champion amateur. I was also hoping to get some good rides in amateur races after last year's successes. However, this proved difficult, and having to turn down good rides in professional races because of the new rule was more than I could bear, so I am taking the plunge and turning professional. I just hope it works out well for me.

Wednesday 30 December

I would already have turned professional by now were it not for the opportunity of a storybook ending to 1987 and also to my amateur career. A month ago Alan Blackmore asked me to ride one of his best horses, Silent Echo, in a race at Warwick today. Mr Blackmore is a permit holder and former amateur rider who trains in Hertfordshire. His operation is very much a family affair – his eldest son Christopher, a vet, also acts as his assistant trainer. Today's race is named in memory of Mr Blackmore's son Michael, who was tragically killed in a racing accident in May 1986. The horse didn't appear to have much chance from its entry in the Racing Calendar, but nonetheless I wanted to preserve my amateur status for a race which was so special to the family.

My older brother Marcus, who I always call Fluffy because of his curly hair, was riding the favourite, Latin American, trained by Captain Tim Forster. The pair of us were upsides in front seven fences from home, but he soon drew ten lengths clear, which did not surprise me as Latin American had hammered Silent Echo by a distance earlier in the season. However, I was determined not to give up, and especially determined to beat Fluffy, a very good amateur rider, if I could.

Prologue

Approaching the last I was still lengths down on Latin
American and the other leaders, but Echo suddenly
started to run and somehow we got up to win by a
narrow margin.

It was absolutely belting with rain as we came into
the winners' enclosure and everyone looked drowned,
but nevertheless we were given a Gold Cup reception
and the atmosphere was fantastic. I was presented with a
beautiful trophy and a magnum of champagne from the
racecourse to mark my last amateur ride. I was deeply
touched and the celebrations rounded off a memorable
day's racing for me. I'm sure it was Michael Blackmore
who gave the old horse a kick at the last, because it sure
as hell wasn't me!

Later on Dad's tearaway, Swift Guide, completed the
course for the first time under a great ride from Martin
Bosley to set the seal on a wonderful day. We travelled
home together in the pouring rain – I only hope the New
Year brings some better weather.

Thursday 31 December

My first day as a professional jockey – watch out, Scu!
Seriously though, turning pro will not affect my attitude
to race-riding, although it will mean a £50 riding fee
for each mount, plus a percentage of any prize-money
earned.

I received both today – I had two rides at Leicester for
John Spearing, who trains at Alcester near Stratford-
upon-Avon, and who regularly puts me up on some
of his horses. The ground was bottomless, but Double
Calibre ran through it well to finish fifth in the novice
hurdle, while Nodalotte won the novice chase to give me
my first professional win.

Strangely enough, I had been rather uncertain about
riding Nodalotte in his first outing of the season at
Warwick a few weeks ago, because of his reputation for
not jumping too well. In fact Mr Spearing had given me
the option of not riding the horse on that occasion, but at

the same time he had said that if he got round he could be
well placed. That, coming from Mr Spearing, for whom
I have a great deal of respect, was good enough for me,
and after today's result I'm glad I didn't back out of the
ride. I'm becoming really attached to Nodalotte and his
funny little ways. He's an ugly, ignorant-looking horse
and nobody else seems to like him, but after today he'll
always be very special to me. He loves being in charge,
and as I can't hold him he knows who's boss!

After my two rides I changed and helped Dad saddle
Promando Lad, Fluffy's mount in the other novice chase.
He's had his training problems, but his jumping is usually
outstanding. Fluffy had him going well approaching the
last fence with a circuit to go when, to quote my brother
later, he was unsighted by another horse and turned a
complete somersault. From my position in the stands I
knew that Fluffy wasn't going to get up too quickly: he
lay motionless and I expected the worst. I tore down the
steps, leaped over two sets of railings and sprinted down
the course. By the time I reached him I was completely
out of breath and my side ached from contact with a
railing I had misjudged.

Fluffy had still not moved, and complained about
his shoulder, although I was relieved to discover that
his back was OK. He was moved gently off the course
and on to the side, where he continued to insist that we
should move him before the horses came round again
and trod all over him! From there he was carried to the
ambulance and taken to the ambulance room, where his
colours and back-pad were carefully removed. This took
about ten minutes and he complained bitterly, although
he insisted that his back-pad should not be cut off. I was
not at all pleased when, again at his insistence, the nurse
drew out her scissors and cut right down the middle
of his sweatshirt. It happened to be my best striped
sweatshirt – I've been searching for it for almost a week
and he must have nicked it!

A possible broken collar-bone was diagnosed, and I
went with Fluffy to Leicester Hospital, where the injury
was confirmed. The nurse helping him had obviously
not dealt with an injured jockey before, for when she

removed his breeches and discovered that underneath
he was wearing nothing but a pair of women's tights
– which all male jockeys do – she asked him if he got
satisfaction from wearing women's clothes. I replied
on his behalf 'No, but he does get satisfaction from
women!'.

There were no other injuries, so when Fluffy had been
strapped up my close friend, conditional jockey Carl
Llewellyn kindly collected us and drove us home. By
this time the patient was beginning to feel that he might
live after all, and began to take the micky out of
Carl's driving abilities. This was a mistake, because Carl
countered by standing violently on the brakes, which
made Fluffy feel that his bone was about to come through
his skin, and soon shut him up.

In his early days of race-riding, before he had ever
ridden a winner, Marcus finished second on Brown
Jock at Plumpton. There was marginal interference by
the winner, although not really enough to affect the
result. Nevertheless, Marcus lodged an objection with
the stewards, and when they asked him why he was
objecting he replied: 'Because Mum told me to'. He was
awarded the race!

My poor brother must have been in some pain, because he
declined an invitation to spend New Year's Eve at our
traditional haunt, the Pound in Goosey.

The evening would not have been the same without
a good session involving some very entertaining characters, including Carl, Martin Bosley and his girlfriend
Sarah Whitaker, Richard Dunwoody and his fiancée Carol
Abraham, and Chris Nash. Martin – often referred to
as 'Mart the Fart' – is one of the most genuine people you could wish to meet, and nothing ever seems
to get to him. His tremendous sense of fun makes
him the ideal companion for Saturday nights and holidays, when we can let our hair down. He is brave,
too – he needs to be as he rides some of Dad's less
reliable novice chasers. 'Woody' is a naturally gifted
rider who has, of course, won just about everything
bar a general election.

Although the jockeys are all dedicated professionals,

they made sure they saw in the New Year in traditional style, never holding an empty glass for very long. I am a non-drinker myself so I acted as chauffeur to several members of the party when we finally wound our way home. I think I deserve sponsorship from Perrier!

January

Friday 1 January

Happy New Year! (though Fluffy probably wouldn't agree). Thank heavens my ride was at Cheltenham today, and not miles away at Catterick or Carlisle. I rode Belinda Vard for Dad in the two-and-a-half-mile novice hurdle. She's a chestnut mare, a type normally renowned for being difficult, but she is an exception to the rule. She ran on well up the hill to finish fourth and I think she'll win a race before the end of the season. The owners are new to the sport and very enthusiastic.

Saturday 2 January

It never seems to stop raining at the moment, and not surprisingly Worcester is off. I had a busy day at home, both in the yard and in my office where I caught up on some letters. Answering all my mail can be tedious, but it's nice to know that people are interested enough in my riding to sit down and take the trouble to write to me. I receive many requests for signed photographs. Some letters are straightforward, some are entertaining and others are really weird. One guy sent me a signed photograph of what he said was himself – it was a picture of a chimpanzee! On another occasion I had a letter from someone who was obviously very distressed. He wrote that he had no job and nothing to live for and that by the time I received his letter he would be dead because he was going to take an overdose. Fortunately, he had put his address on the letter and I alerted the police, who found that he had, in fact, taken the overdose, but they were able to get him to hospital in time for him to be saved. That was quite a spooky experience. Many people who write say that they saw me at the races but were too shy or embarrassed to approach me – I never knew I was that frightening!

Now that I have turned professional I can pursue possible sponsorship deals. Last season Dick Lovett, a BMW dealer in Swindon, approached me about a sponsored car, but because of my amateur status I couldn't accept it. I rang him this morning, and I hope something comes of it this time.

Fluffy is still dying. He and his best friends Paint and Jessica (his terrier and lurcher) have taken over my room, as the bed is more comfortable and the stereo works.

On Saturdays, as there is no racing the next day, jockeys can relax and have a few drinks and a good meal for once. This evening a group of us went to the Pound in Goosey again, and as usual there was rarely a dull moment. I think some people in racing are the funniest people in the world. Everyone is so down to earth and we all share the same hobby – laughing. When people like Martin Bosley are in good form, scriptwriters for radio and television might do well to listen to them.

Sunday 3 January

I coughed non-stop last night and hardly slept a wink, and I felt very groggy when I rode out this morning. I have also lost my voice, which could not have happened at a worse time, because this evening I was due to record

a round of the ITV quiz programme *Sporting Triangles*,
which will be broadcast at a later date. I left home
at 3.00 pm in a chauffeured car which I shared with
John Francome, who was recording a separate episode
of the programme tonight. I was teamed up with the
footballer Andy Gray, and we finished second. I managed
to get a few questions right, although I was stumped
by a racing one. That was a bit embarrassing, even
though I could have been forgiven as it was about
Flat racing.

Later on, however, when we were all having a drink after
the recording, I made two rather more serious gaffes. First,
I asked Andy Gray when he had retired from football,
which of course he hasn't, then I asked Bryan Robson
what sport he was involved in! At first he thought I
was trying to be funny. After that I decided to be seen
and not heard, and tucked into the buffet provided. I
quite enjoy doing these television quiz programmes
– it's a boost to the ego – but I must confess that my
knowledge of sport in general is not as good as it might
be.

Monday 4 January

Racing was on at Newbury today. It was still raining
and the ground was terrible, so Captain Forster took
out Polar Sunset, which I was due to ride. However,
I did ride Sunbeam Talbot, normally Fluffy's mount,
in the novice chase. He was quite well fancied and
I had him well up, but his jumping wasn't great
and I was unseated at the last ditch while we were
still in front. We both returned in one piece, but I
took a lot of stick from Fluffy and the others, and
no doubt gave the watching press photographers
a good picture. On the way home the rain tipped
down, and I'll be surprised if there is any racing
tomorrow.

Tuesday 5 January

I was right. All racing was off today and prospects for the rest of the week don't look good. Neither does the prospect of my bank balance being swelled by riding fees.

It was a pretty routine day. I got soaked riding out three lots this morning, and later helped out with evening stables. This evening I had a game of squash with Bob Andrews, one of Captain Forster's lads. Despite the fact that he puts up a bit of overweight he annihilated me as usual.

Riding out is something that jockeys do most days of the week, and of course it is a vital part of a horse's training programme. Someone like Richard Dunwoody, who is attached to David Nicholson's yard, will ride out there most mornings, but because I'm not based in one particular yard I travel all over the place to ride out. For example, the trip to Mr Mitchell's yard is 100 miles, which sometimes means a 5.00 am start.

You normally arrive at the yard at around 7.00 am, and there will be a notice in the tack room listing the riders along with the horses each will be exercising. You are given the tack by the head lad, unless the horse has already been tacked up, although I usually take my own saddle with me.

Each string pulls out of the yard at a set time. You may have been told the night before that you are schooling a horse over fences because it is due to run in a few days' time, but usually you walk up to the gallops not knowing what you'll be doing. When you reach the gallops the trainer will give you your instructions. You do a short warm up and are then put in pairs, and told how fast to go, where to pull up and so on. If you are schooling a horse you will be told how many fences or hurdles to jump. If you are just working a horse, that is exercising it, you will be told how far to gallop. Distances vary from trainer to trainer: Terry Casey often gallops his horses over two miles; other perhaps just a few furlongs.

Once you have finished schooling a horse you might change immediately on to another one while one of the stable lads takes the first horse back to the yard, or you may ride the horse back yourself. You wash off its legs and saddle marks, put a rug on it and make sure it has hay and water. This routine is repeated with the next lot.

Wednesday 6 January

Although racing was off again today I still had to be up before dawn, leaving home at 5.30 this morning to ride work at John Spearing's yard at Alcester, on the other side of Stratford-upon-Avon. I allowed myself plenty of time, as my sense of direction is not too good, but today the trip was undramatic and I had time to stop and read the *Sporting Life* before arriving at Mr Spearing's at 7.15. Work went well, and Nodalotte seems to have recovered from his race at Leicester.

Back at home I was interviewed by John Karter of the *Independent*. While I do appreciate the value of publicity, I sometimes wish I could be left alone to concentrate on my riding. The publicity I am given is totally out of proportion to my ability as a rider – I honestly believe that if I were a man I would be given little or none at all.

Thursday 7 January

Racing resumed at Lingfield today. I took the ride on Bold King's Hussar because Fluffy still needs a few more days to recover from his shoulder injury. The ground was desperate but my horse went through it well to win by a couple of lengths. Fluffy declared himself to be 'as sick as a parrot' at missing a winner, but he knows that sometimes these things can work to his advantage: his ride on Brown Veil in last year's Grand National came about only because both Mark Dwyer and myself were injured. My win today put me one in front of Diane Clay for the ladies' title.

Friday 8 January

There has been more rain and all racing was off once
again. The *Sporting Life* carried a typically pessimistic
quote from Dad about Bold King's Hussar's win yesterday. He said that the heavy ground suited the horse,
who is probably very slow anyway. Dad always looks on
the bright side of life, bless him! Luckily the owner,
Mrs David Plunkett, took Dad's words in good spirit,
although they certainly can't have done her ego any
good.

I was due to ride Chelsea Man for Dai Williams at
Haydock today, and even though the horse is not the
soundest of jumpers I was looking forward to it because
whenever I have been down to ride this novice chaser the
fates have conspired to stop me. I was very offended on
one occasion when the owners thought I didn't want to
take my chance on the horse, when I had in fact got off
it because I was so sore from an earlier fall that I didn't
think I could do it justice. Today, then, I had something
to prove, but sure enough the jinx persisted, this time in
the shape of the weather.

Still no word from Dick Lovett in Swindon, and my
own car doesn't sound very healthy.

Saturday 9 January

Warwick was off, which was particularly annoying today
because I was due to have my first ride for Anabel King,
on Visual Identity in the novice chase. He's only had two
runs over fences but his form over hurdles has suggested
that he could run really well. Also, I'm always keen to
ride for a trainer I haven't ridden for previously – if the
race goes well it leads to more rides.

I rode work at John Spearing's this morning and this
afternoon watched a bit of Sandown on the box. John
Karter's article in the *Independent* was all right except for

one stupid 'quote', which I didn't even say: 'It gives me a real buzz to go out for a race knowing I'm on a one-way ticket'. He must be joking! No jockey wants to fall.

We had a great Saturday night at the Rat's Castle in Faringdon. With Michael Caulfield – known to everyone as Corky – on the team we were guaranteed a good night. Corky, a great friend of Fluffy's, is not actually involved in racing, although he is Martin Bosley's lodger. He turns his hand to a number of things, although he does none of them very well as yet! He loves racing and hopes that one day he will make a living out of the sport in one capacity or another. He also spends a great deal of time asking for lifts to the races and even more time apologising for doing so! Also there tonight were Woody and Carol, Martin and Sarah, Fluffy and girlfriend, Carl, Brendan Powell and Lorna Vincent, and Woody's sister Gail.

Brendan, a very hard-working freelance jockey, is a natural lightweight who eats tons of junk food and smokes endless packets of revolting cigarettes. He is a teetotaller like me, and is addicted to Coca-Cola – he drinks at least two litres of it a day. He shares a house with Lorna, the first really successful lady jockey.

Sunday 10 January

Today was officially my Sunday off, but as usual Dad and I went through the entries together this morning. Dad noticed the sudden drop in entries I'd suggested for amateurs-only races, whereas before the New Year I would have made sure that these races were well-filled with entries from our stable. After we've finished Mum checks the entries to make sure we haven't made any mistakes, such as putting a gelding in a mares-only race, or a five-year-old in a four-year-old race.

Then began a round of interviews. The first was at 11.00 am, for a fitness magazine. They stayed until 1.30 pm, spending ages in a gym taking photographs of me wearing some dreadful black

and yellow cycling shorts, and then taking endless
shots of me standing in the yard in my colours.
This seemed ridiculous, as the only place you ever
see a jockey wearing colours is on the racecourse.
Once, I was even photographed humping hay in my
colours!

At 2.00 pm the *Reading Evening Post* arrived to
take more pictures, which meant that I missed
Sunday lunch at Martin Bosley's, and at 4.00 pm I
had to record a taped interview with a local radio
station. Relieved that the day's P.R. work was
over at last, I looked at my diary to double-check
that I was free, and was aghast to read '5.30 pm:
interview: *Gay News*'. For a split second I fell
for it, before I recognised the hands of Fluffy and
Corky!

In the evening I played squash with Chris Maude,
another lad from Captain Forster's yard, and this time
I was victorious. Finally, I retired to a warm room to
watch a video of Lionel Richie live, during which I fell
fast asleep.

Monday 11 January

Both Chepstow and Wolverhampton were abandoned
today, which gave me the opportunity to 'phone Dick
Lovett Garages and arrange to go and talk to them about
a sponsored car.

It's very frustrating when a meeting is abandoned
due to weather, especially if you have a good ride lined
up. The next time it runs you may not be available
to ride it, and if another jockey does well on it, he or
she may keep the ride. Cancellations also mean the
loss of riding fees, of course. But there's no point in
getting too upset, because there's nothing you can
do about it except to pray for an improvement in the
weather.

Tuesday 12 January

Newton Abbot was on today, although the ground was so desperately heavy that one fence on the chase circuit was omitted. I rode Regal Nod in the mares-only novice hurdle, and although we made all the early running we fell at the sixth. So that was four and a half hours' driving for a fall – it's not only the weather that makes jump racing a frustrating business! I had a hot bath to ease the bruising, and an early night.

Wednesday 13 January

Plumpton was abandoned and I was able to keep my appointment with Dick Lovett Garages. They have BMW and Peugeot agencies and I expected to be given one of the small Peugeot 205s, but instead they're going to give me a BMW 316. In addition, they will change the car regularly, and pay all the road tax and servicing costs, so all I have to worry about is insurance and petrol. In return, I have to attend about a dozen of their social functions a year, one of them at a big race meeting, which this year will be the Cheltenham Festival in March. All in all I think I have been given a very good deal, and I'm deeply indebted to Dick Lovett. Until now I've driven my faithful Ford Escort, which somehow doesn't quite live up to a BMW. I am particularly pleased that the car will be changed regularly, as my driving tends to be a little on the unpredictable side – no doubt the BMW will be pulled out of a ditch sooner or later.

Of course, I'm delighted to have a sponsored car, but I can imagine the remarks that will come my way whenever I wear the jumper with the immortal words 'Dick Lovett' printed across a rather obvious part of my anatomy.

Thursday 14 January

It was quite a good day really, with only an hour's drive
to Wincanton and no extra bruises to show for it. I had
two rides, one of which was satisfactory and the other
best forgotten. Sir Kenwin ran his best race of the season
to finish fourth, and I then rode a horse called Too Late,
owned by Nora Carroll, who supplied my first-ever
outside ride, which was coincidentally also my first-ever
winner.

It is said that certain horses run well for certain
jockeys, and also that certain horses don't, and the latter
was certainly true of Too Late and me. He was never
confident, he wouldn't jump, I didn't like him and we
finished a well-beaten last. Maybe he had an off day, but
whatever the situation Dad was not best pleased, and no
doubt someone else will have the mount next time out.
This is one of the disadvantages of riding for a family
stable – it must look most odd to partisan spectators
when you're jocked off a horse by your own father.

Friday 15 January

When I first schooled Prime Number for Dad he was on
his worst behaviour, and I was praying that he wouldn't
make a complete idiot out of me today at Henrietta
Knight's place. She has a livery yard at Lockinge near
Wantage, and also trains a few point-to-pointers. She has
really good facilities which quite a lot of trainers use from
time to time. Thankfully, he co-operated this morning
and jumped outstandingly well, establishing himself as a
possible Cheltenham runner.

I'm going to sell my rather battered Ford Escort
when my BMW is ready, so I took it in for its
MOT. It passed, but not without requiring a bit of
work.

Saturday 16 January

The weather continues to be foul and racing was off
again. What should have been an exciting Saturday at
Ascot therefore turned out to be a rather dull day, and I
had to be content with riding work at Peter Cundell's.
Mr Cundell trains in Compton, the next village to East
Ilsley, and has handled a stack of good horses on the
Flat as well as over the jumps. His big wins include the
King George VI Chase, the Hennessy Cognac Gold Cup
and the Mackeson Gold Cup. Still, it presented a rare
opportunity to spend some time on my own, a luxury
which I appreciate. At this time of year the video works
overtime, which is more than I'm doing. Today I spent
some time criticising myself on past videos, and watching
one of Scu riding to see how it's properly done. I also
spent some time on the telephone trying to arrange a lift
to Carlisle on Monday, where I have accepted the ride on
Rebecca's Pet for Gerry Kelly, who has a small yard at
Sheriff Hutton in Yorkshire.

Sunday 17 January

Nobody from this area is going to Carlisle tomorrow
so I'm stuck with a ten-hour round trip in my own
company, and I hate driving. But it still beats staying at
home without a ride.

Monday 18 January

Gerry Kelly is a lovely man but I'm afraid I can't say
the same about all his horses. Rebecca's Pet, a small mare
who had previously run on the Flat with no success, almost
knocked me out when she reared her head up at the
start, and was reluctant to line up. We eventually pulled
up two out when tailed off, and I was the butt of a lot of

leg-pulling for going all the way to Carlisle for a ride like that. Much sooner Carlisle than no ride at all!

The most remarkable feat of the day as far as I'm concerned is that I found Carlisle at all, because my sense of direction is, as I have already mentioned, useless. Fluffy still delights in reminding me of the time when I set off from Compton, our neighbouring village, to Newbury, our nearest main town. I had made the journey from East Ilsley to Newbury countless times, but never from Compton. True to form, I managed to get lost, and had to ring home for directions. Now you can see why I'm amazed I found Carlisle!

Tuesday 19 January

This morning I schooled Roving Glen, who is due to run at Windsor tomorrow, and later on Graham Owen, a researcher from *Wogan*, came to talk to me. I'm going to be on the programme just before the National, and already I'm dreading it. Graham's job is to meet prospective guests well in advance and to find out a little about them and about their backgrounds so that suitable questions can be prepared for the programme itself.

Wednesday 20 January

An encouraging day. Roving Glen has always acted on firm going in the past, and we thought that today's heavy ground would not suit him. By halfway we were tailed off, and I feared the worst, but he got into his stride again and ran on well to finish third, absolutely flying at the end. He is certain to improve next time out, especially as he has been off the track since October, and I think he'll win a race before too long. I only hope I do the same.

Thursday 21 January

Lingfield was on today, although the ground was desperate. Because of this the stewards cut out the last hurdle, but I think it would have been better to have left it in, as we were left with a very long run in.

I rode Bold King's Hussar, who won for me at the same course two weeks ago. He went through the ground well and we won again, but the prize-money for our efforts was the princely sum of £400! Dad was absolutely furious, and stated publicly that this was a disgrace for a course like Lingfield. His outburst has obviously had some effect, because the course authorities have said that in future no race will be worth less than £1,000.

Apart from Bold King's Hussar's victory the day was not a notable one for the Armytage stable. I rode a horse called You Can Be Sure, owned by Miss Susan Thomson. She's a good jumper, bought from Ireland, but on this occasion something was wrong and I had to pull her up early on and walk back. Martin Bosley rode Brown Gambler in the next, but pulled up, and Hywel Davies did the same with Ronald's Carole in the handicap chase. This was especially disappointing as Ronald's Carole is a good handicapper who stays well on soft ground and was placed in all his outings last season. But there are days when horses, like humans, are below par, and this was one of them. At least we didn't return home totally empty-handed.

Friday 22 January

I was due to ride Sir Kenwin at Towcester but the meeting was called off. Instead I diverted to Kempton Park to ride Flemington for Bill Perrin. Although we weren't actually in the shake-up when it mattered, the horse ran encouragingly.

Saturday 23 January

There was some doubt about Haydock being on today, and a mid-morning inspection was planned. I set off in the hope of a ride with Steve Taylor of the *Sporting Life* and Nicky Henderson's talented conditional jockey, Jamie Osborne. On the way we stopped at a motorway service station and Steve went to telephone the course to find out about prospects. He came back with the news that the meeting was still on, so we set off up the motorway to continue our journey. But at the next junction he turned round and headed south again. The meeting had been abandoned, and Steve was having us on! This meant that yet again I missed riding Chelsea Man, and although he's not the safest conveyance I still feel I have something to prove to the owners.

As it was a Saturday, when jockeys with weight problems can indulge themselves slightly, a group of us consisting of Carl and myself, Woody and Carol, and Henry Candy's assistant, Richard Phillips, went into Oxford in the evening for a pizza. Although I don't have the same weight problems as some of my male colleagues, who have to spend endless hours in the sauna, I do watch what I eat, and I certainly don't live on hamburgers and pizzas all the time. There was a stage when I weighed just over ten stones, but now I'm steady at just under nine. If he were a racehorse, Richard would draw from the tipsters the comment 'never one to be left out of the calculations, but has been known to behave badly at the start'. When he's in good form he's great company. He has a burning desire to train horses and is always thinking of ways of keeping in touch with potential owners. Naturally amusing, his impressions of racing characters are quite brilliant. Perhaps he should forget about training and go on the stage.

Sunday 24 January

Chris Hawkins came over this morning to interview me
for the March issue of *Pacemaker*, and later on I played
squash with Peter Fisher in Hungerford. Peter was
one of the people who helped Bob Champion regain
fitness when he was recovering from cancer a few years
ago.

Monday 25 January

I left home at 5.30 this morning for Nigel Tinkler's
yard at Malton in North Yorkshire where I was to school
Darkorjon for the first time. This was the horse Nigel's
father, Colin, one of racing's greatest characters, had
bought to replace the ill-fated The Ellier for his Full
Circle Syndicate. Darkorjon is my intended Grand National
mount this year so there is naturally a lot of interest
in our partnership, not least because the horse cost
so much. The schooling session, which would normally
have been a quiet affair, was attended by a number of the
racing press who have little else to write about during
this wet month.
   It was a very foggy morning, which was just as
well as it turned out. Darkorjon and I fell at the
first obstacle we jumped together – a great start to a
Grand National preparation. He proceeded to gallop past
the corps of press waiting at the top of the schooling
ground. They had not seen the fall and Colin, who
is at his best in a tricky situation, told them that the
loose horse was in fact the lead horse, not Darkorjon.
He told me to keep quiet about the incident and we
were eventually reunited and jumped without mishap the
second time. I spent the rest of the day with the Tinklers
before driving back to Berkshire in the late afternoon.

Tuesday 26 January

All racing was off today, so I went to Dick Lovett's in
Swindon to collect my sponsored BMW. It looks very
smart in white, and the *Racing Post* were there to take
photographs. Thankfully they haven't painted my name
all over the car, preferring what is known in the business
as subtle sponsorship.

Later on Carl and I set off to see *Fatal Attraction*,
which is the big film at the moment, but the queue was
enormous so we went to McDonald's instead.

Thursday 28 January

I was offered the ride on Polar Sunset for Captain
Forster at Huntingdon but Nodalotte was down to
run at Taunton so I went there instead. In the event,
Huntingdon was off anyway. The ground was very soft,
but the horse jumped immaculately and we led all the
way, winning quite easily, even though I did nearly fall
off at the last!

Today is Martin Bosley's birthday, which called for a
celebration supper at his house in the evening.

Friday 29 January

I was to ride Mac's Gold at Wincanton today, but the
weather intervened once again.

Saturday 30 January

I rode Prime Number for Dad in the two-mile novice
hurdle at Cheltenham today. We finished seventh, in
front of Just Acquitted, and although he missed the last
hurdle my horse ran promisingly. All being well, he'll

be entered for the supreme novice hurdle at the Festival meeting in March.

This evening I had supper at Fluffy's house. As is his wont he had asked loads of people, but it had not occurred to him to go out and buy anything to feed them with, so we ended up with take-away pizzas!

Sunday 31 January

Although today was officially my weekly day off, I was nevertheless happy to go over to Bradfield to be photographed handing over a cheque for heart research. I'm often asked to present prizes, open shops or appear at dinners and other charity functions. I'm always glad to help out with charity events whenever I can.

January has been a dreadful month weather-wise, and I only hope February is an improvement.

February

Monday 1 February

When you have a good ride booked it is doubly frustrating for racing to be abandoned. I had two in prospect
at Southwell today, Silent Echo and What, but all racing
was off due to more rain. I had to content myself with
riding out until noon, when George Selwyn arrived to
take some photographs for *Pacemaker*.

Because the National is only two months away, and
the foul weather is preventing me from getting much
race-riding, I have decided to start an extra fitness
campaign. In the summer months I swim, run, play squash
and do weight training, but now it will be mainly squash
and running. I hate swimming in the cold weather and
I only do weight training when I can do it on a regular
basis, three times a week. I like running on the downs,
through the paddocks, jumping any obstacle that comes
my way, as this keeps up the interest. But if it's dark I
just run round the village, to avoid the bogeymen on the
downs.

My BMW was due for a service today and Dick
Lovett's garage had arranged to collect it. I left it
unlocked outside the house, and when the man arrived at
10.00 am I gave him the keys and told him where it was.
A few minutes later he was back, saying it wasn't there.

Embarrassed, I explained that I'd left the keys on the kitchen table, and that Mum must have taken the other set of keys and borrowed the car to go shopping. At this point our head lad, Gordon Cramp, came in and told me the police were looking for me. They had towed the car away, he said, because a few days previously a hidden camera on a bridge over the M4 had recorded me doing 100 mph. By now I was becoming alarmed, and the man from the garage was muttering about straining the engine when the car was still being run in. Just for a moment it occurred to me that Gordon was telling the truth, but then a particularly dozy Irish lad, who won't be with us for much longer, stuck his head through the window and said he'd put the car in the tractor shed out of the way. It was a great feat in itself for him to find the tractor shed in the first place.

People seem to enjoy winding me up like this!

Tuesday 2 February

Yet another blank day. Colin Tinkler, who keeps me very well-informed about my Grand National mount Darkorjon, rang to tell me of his latest plans for the horse. He has been declared for Wetherby and Sandown on Saturday, but if he doesn't run at either of those meetings he may well go to Ascot the following Wednesday. After that he may have one more race before Cheltenham, where he will run in either the Gold Cup or the Kim Muir. If he goes in the latter Fluffy will ride him, as it's an amateurs-only race. Colin's 'phone call reminded me that I have also been offered the ride on Gee-A in the National, and I must make a decision soon.

After an interview with Richard Onslow for the Cheltenham programme I went for a run, and took a right pearler tripping over a gate on to Dad's all-weather strip. I cut my hand quite badly, so I declined the offer of a game of squash with Bob Andrews, and went shopping in Newbury instead.

I just hope there's some racing again soon!

Wednesday 3 February

Windsor is waterlogged. I was due to go there to ride Sir
Kenwin for Dad and Polar Sunset for Captain Forster.
I thoroughly enjoy riding Polar Sunset: he's a brilliant
jumper and you can ask him to come up from anywhere.
I'm really annoyed at missing two such good rides.

Still, the rain has eased up and it looks as though
Towcester and Lingfield will both be on tomorrow.
At present I have booked rides at both meetings, so I
must have a good chance of at least getting a ride round
tomorrow! I'm booked to ride Mac's Gold for Dad at
Towcester, where there is a 7.30 am inspection, and two
lesser horses at Lingfield, where no inspection is planned.
I get very frustrated when there is no racing, and any ride
will be better than nothing at the moment.

Thursday 4 February

Towcester was called off early, but Lingfield went ahead,
so I arranged a lift there with Brendan Powell and Charlie
Mann. I was down to ride two hurdlers for Gerry Kelly,
for whom I made that fruitless trip to Carlisle two weeks
ago. Gerry trains near York, works extremely hard, and
deserves better horses as a reward. He drove the horses
down himself yesterday.

I'm very good at sleeping in cars and I was snoozing
happily soon after Brendan collected me. I slept soundly
until we were nearly at Lingfield, when I was awoken by
some furious cursing and swearing from the front seats.
Bob Kington, who acts as agent to several jockeys in the
Lambourn area and books their rides, had just been on
the carphone to tell Brendan and Charlie that the meeting
had been abandoned after all. We turned for home,
thoroughly fed up, and pigged ourselves at a Kentucky
Fried Chicken on the way.

I went for a long run this afternoon before settling down to do some office work and to sort out future rides. Darkorjon will not now run on Saturday – the weather is still dicey and Colin Tinkler does not want to take him all the way to Sandown only to find that racing is off. Furthermore Nigel Tinkler is, quite rightly, against running him until the National weights are published, in case he should run well and go up a few pounds. So for the sake of a few days we will wait, and he will probably now run at Ascot next Wednesday.

In company with Carl and Martin I spent the evening at Woody's house, watching a particularly gory video called *Lethal Weapon*. All tomorrow's card are already abandoned.

Friday 5 February

With another tedious day in prospect it was good to have my spirits lifted by an amusing letter from Corky Caulfield, who is in Ireland. He is working for a trainer in County Waterford, where he says it rains continuously and he can't understand a word the locals are saying. He's been there ten days now and hopes to get a ride in a point-to-point soon. No one believes him.

Saturday 6 February

Racing went ahead at Sandown, but needless to say my rides would have been at either Wetherby or Stratford, both of which were off. I rode out Roving Glen first lot, and he seems to have improved tremendously since his run at Windsor. I believe he'll win next time if the right race comes up for him.

I spent a lazy afternoon watching television. Woody rode an outstanding treble at Sandown on Long Engagement, Charter Party and Celtic Chief, and I don't think anyone would dispute the fact that he's a real pleasure to watch. Carol was there, so I expect she was having kittens in the stand – she gets very excited when Woody is involved in a finish.

I met up with them later, along with Martin, Sarah, Carl, Bob Kington and his wife Helen, Brendan and Chris Nash and we spent the evening celebrating Woody's successful day at the Dragon Inn, a Chinese restaurant in Burford. We had a great time and ate far too much, especially Martin, who has to do ten stone on Monday. Some hope, I suspect.

Sunday 7 February

Officially this was my Sunday off, but as usual I went through the entries with Dad. At 10.00 am two men from TVS arrived to discuss a half-hour programme they are making about me, which will be broadcast on the eve of the Grand National. The cameras will follow me around for eight days, so the end product will depend on what sort of a week I have.

I schooled a filly called Merryett over some small hurdles this afternoon. She's a four-year-old from Belgium who has run a few times on the Flat. She jumps well when she meets the hurdles on a long stride, but as yet she seems unaware that when she gets close to them she must shorten her stride and fold up in front. She has a great temperament, though, and by the end of the session she was beginning to get the idea. I hope she'll do well on the racecourse because she has some very nice owners who are new to us this season.

Bob Andrews arrived today from Captain Forster's yard, and in two weeks' time will take over as head lad from Gordon Cramp. Gordon is leaving us after 13 years to go to Philip Hobbs in the West Country, and everyone will miss him a lot.

Monday 8 February

Racing was off again today, but for once I wasn't
too disappointed. I was due to ride Bladon Park for Dad
at Fontwell and I wasn't relishing the prospect. The horse
is a bad jumper, and she fell when I rode her in a
novice chase at Warwick last November, treading all over
my thigh and causing extensive cuts and bruising. So
I was quite happy to play squash with Chris Maude and
help out at evening stables before joining former jockey
Anthony Webber and his wife Jayne for supper. I imagine
Martin was quite relieved racing was off, too. After
pigging himself on Saturday night I doubt if he would
have made the ten stone he was due to do today, and
would surely have put up a few pounds overweight!

Tuesday 9 February

Another wasted day. I had to get up at 5.15 am to 'phone
John Spearing about going over there to school, but
he said it was just too windy. To make matters worse
Warwick was off, so all I could do was ride out at home.

However, prospects for Ascot tomorrow are good, and
Darkorjon is a confirmed runner. Geoff Hubbard also
has two in the first and I've been asked to ride one of
them, Earl Soham. Mr Hubbard is a permit holder who,
assisted by Ferdie Murphy, trains several good horses,
including Gee-A, whom I rode to victory at the Festival
meeting last year and whom I have been asked to ride in
this year's National. The fact that the horse is called Gee-
A is pure coincidence and nothing to do with me – they
are Mr Hubbard's initials. All in all it should be a very
interesting and exciting day, with my National mount
from Ireland running in England for the first time and the
opportunity to renew my partnership with Mr Hubbard,
for whom I rode so many winners last year.

First, though, I had to extricate myself from a bad
muddle I have created by accepting two rides in the first,

Just Acquitted for Jim Mahon as well as Earl Soham for Mr Hubbard. Perhaps I misunderstood and thought they were to run in different races, but in any event it was embarrassing. My embarrassment was made more acute by the fact that I have already had to get off Just Acquitted on a previous occasion in order to ride for Dad.

Eventually I opted for Mr Hubbard's horse, mainly because I don't want to jeopardise my chances of riding Gee-A for him at Cheltenham and Aintree. Fluffy will ride Just Acquitted: he is now back in one piece, living life to the full again, and is eagerly awaiting a good ride. Nevertheless, Mr Mahon is not at all impressed by the way I've handled things!

Wednesday 10 February

Racing is a great leveller, and today was a perfect example. It started full of excitement and eager anticipation and ended in disaster. Instead of celebrating what I hoped would be a successful first run in England for Darkorjon, I am nursing a broken collar-bone and feeling thoroughly sorry for myself.

When I arrived at Ascot this morning the press were waiting for me with numerous questions about the horse, so I was glad to get away to go out for the first race. The ground was soft and Earl Soham, a great big, backward, weak baby, jumped immaculately. I think he'll be a very nice horse one day. Then I had a two-race gap before the big one, which gave me plenty of time to talk to Colin and Nigel Tinkler, both of whom had made the long journey down from Malton.

Darkorjon looked 110 per cent fit in the paddock, and he felt good going to the start. Nigel had instructed me to give him plenty of room early on – if everyone was lining up down the inner I should go down the outer, and vice versa. He also told me not to hurry too early, so we set off near the back. Passing the stands with a circuit to go I felt that we weren't going too well, but

February

I hadn't realised just how much was left in the tank.
Darkorjon was simply lobbing along, nicely switched
off, so I moved him up a few places, and having seen
some daylight he became very keen. He also began to
hang strongly to the right, so I took him up past the
first two horses to get him on the rails. Looking back,
I believe I was right to go for the rails, but I should
have stayed behind the two leaders instead of going in
front.

He was going as well as anything as we approached
the last ditch, which is four from home, and I felt we
had a good chance. He met the fence a little close, and I
tried to help him by shortening his stride, but to no avail:
he just fired me straight into the ground. After I had
recovered from the initial shock of being catapulted from
the saddle I thought I had been lucky enough to escape
with a winding. But my relief was short-lived: as I stood
up I felt considerable discomfort in my left shoulder, the
ominous sign of a broken collar-bone. I was returned to
the ambulance room where Dr Michael Allen, the Jockey
Club Medical Officer, confirmed the break. Although I
was not in any desperate pain, I burst into tears when he
signed me off for three weeks! I should have been grateful
that it was only a collar-bone and that I was side-lined
for only three weeks, because it could have been a great
deal worse.

Next I was taken to the nearby Heatherwood Hospital
to be X-rayed and strapped up. The waiting room there
looked more like a weighing room, with trainers such
as Josh Gifford and Philip Hobbs collecting injured
jockeys after some carnage in the last. Carl and Fluffy
came for me, and we 'phoned Mum to ask her to
arrange an appointment as soon as possible with John
Skull, a specialist in bone injuries who has put quite a
few jockeys back into the saddle quickly after injury.
The appointment with Mr Skull was fixed for 7.30 this
evening at his Swindon surgery, and Carl drove me
there. After a quick examination Mr Skull decided that
the shoulder needed to be pulled back to get the two
overlaps to rejoin again, after which he would bandage
tightly in a figure-of-eight to keep them in place.

As he began to work the pain became unbearable,
but I gritted my teeth, determined to get through it.
I was very near to passing out – I could not support
myself in the chair. I was given a huge red sick bowl
and quickly covered the bottom of it; then I drank a
glass of water and that soon came back up again as well.
I passed out for a while, then recovered, and once
Mr Skull had finished and I was strapped up I felt rela-
tively comfortable.

Meanwhile Carl was having problems of his own.
Sitting in the waiting room, he could hear all the gasps
and groans coming from the surgery and began to feel
faint himself. Eventually he could stand it no longer, and
decided to go back and wait in the car, which was
parked out of earshot 50 yards away. But, weak at the
knees, he didn't make it, and collapsed in a heap in
a soaking wet alleyway. Meanwhile, a lady reported to
the receptionist that there was a drunk outside in the
driveway! He recovered, but as I came out of the surgery
he looked in worse shape than I did: white as a sheet, his
once-immaculate racing clothes filthy dirty, shaking like
a leaf and trying to explain to the nurse what he'd done
with the car keys.

So it was two rather shaken characters who made
their way back to East Ilsley. Carl begged me not to tell
anyone what had happened to him. It was only some
days later, and after a great deal of persuasion, that I was
given permission to reveal all here.

This seemingly endless day was still not over. When
I got home, I had a long telephone conversation with
Colin Tinkler about the day's disaster during which I
rather over-reacted and became very upset. Apparently
Nigel had criticised me for hitting the front so soon, and
in view of what had happened it was now possible that
we would not run in the National, owing to the horse's
inexperience. It made me feel that I had let down not
only myself, but also the Tinklers and the whole Full
Circle team as well, and Mum had to escort a very
unhappy daughter to bed.

As I said, racing is a great leveller with its highs and
lows, but I have never before let any individual day at the

races get me down, so this must not either. It is only a sport after all, and I am determined to get over the day's disappointment as quickly as it was thrust upon me.

Thursday 11 February

I have been inundated with telephone calls from people enquiring after my health, and pressmen wanting the full story, as well as other people calling in at the house, so the day has passed by very quickly. I am pretty helpless at the moment, and had to be bathed and dressed by a very patient aunt. I have a phobia about smelling, but washing under the armpits with this contraption tied round them is difficult, so I settled for half a tin of deodorant instead. The numerous 'phone calls and bunches of flowers have made me feel better already, and I am determined not to take a lie-down-and-die attitude towards the injury, as Fluffy admitted he did after his fall at Leicester on New Year's Eve.

The worst thing about the day was missing three good rides at Huntingdon: John O'Dee for Mr Hubbard; Dad's Prime Number, the horse that has already won for me this season; and Polar Sunset for Captain Forster. It seems that I am destined never to ride that horse!

Friday 12 February

Keeping to my vow not to lie around the house feeling sorry for myself, I went instead to Newbury races today and thoroughly enjoyed myself in the company of Hywel Davies' wife Rachael and their two young children, James and Philippa. Like most jockeys I don't really enjoy going racing unless I'm taking part, but I do like to go along if the family has a runner, or if Fluffy or Carl are riding. Otherwise I stay away, except for meetings like Aintree and Cheltenham. Ronald's Carole was representing Dad today. He is normally a difficult

animal, but Brendan Powell gave him a brilliant ride
and was beaten by Course Hunter only in a photograph.
Brendan certainly earned every penny of his riding fee.

Saturday 13 February

The worst thing about being side-lined is missing
winners, and not being able to ride really hit me for the
first time today. This was because two of my favourite
rides, Nodalotte and Silent Echo, were both due to run at
Uttoxeter. Both were fancied and both would have been
my mounts. In the event, because of the continuing foul
weather, Echo was a non-runner, while Nodalotte, 5–2
favourite and five lengths clear four fences from home
with Peter Dever deputising for me, was eventually
beaten into third place.

Over at Newbury there was cause for great cel-
ebration when Brendan won the Tote Gold Trophy on
Jamesmead, his first big win. The conditions were awful but
I should think Brendan and the horse, both being
Irish, loved slogging through the mud!

At the end of the day I reflected that you don't realise
just how much you miss doing something until you
cannot actually do it, and it makes me wonder how I will
ever satisfy my need to keep the adrenalin going when
my racing days are over.

Tuesday 16 February

I went to Towcester with Carl where Dad had two
runners – Mac's Gold, on which Fluffy finished second,
and Bladon Park, which fell at the last in the novice
chase. So all in all I didn't miss much. We stopped for
supper at the trainer Mark Wilkinson's on the way home.

Wednesday 17 February

While I spent a busy day at home Stuart Shilston,
one of the most under-used and under-rated jockeys,
rode Promando Lad for us at Folkestone. He fell, but
Regal Nod ran well to finish second over two miles at
Worcester. I think she needs two and a half miles – she
could well be a winner for me when I come back.

Thursday 18 February

Decision time. By Sunday I have to let Mr Hubbard
know whether or not I can ride Gee-A for him in the
National. If I say yes I can also ride him at Cheltenham.
But this has created a dilemma for me because no firm
decision has yet been made about Darkorjon's future
programme, including the chance of him running at
Aintree. It seems very early to be asking for a decision,
with the National still almost two months away, but
Mr Hubbard is the boss so I will have to do some hard
thinking over the next few days.

Fluffy won on Accarine today, which puts him at the
top of the amateur jockeys' table.

Saturday 20 February

Dad had two runners in the novice chase at Windsor,
Brown Gambler and Paddy Buskins. Brown Gambler
is a terrific character and a great favourite of mine, since
he's a half-brother to my first-ever race ride, Brown
Jock. I made my debut seven years ago in an amateur
riders' hurdle at Ascot. Brown Jock was an experienced
handicapper and I had ridden him out regularly at home;
so he was a good first ride in public. Paddy Buskins, on
the other hand, reminds me of an overgrown Thelwell
pony, and usually runs like one, too! In the event Brown

Gambler fell, while Paddy Buskins ran quite well under an inspired ride from Martin, who has recently acquired the new nickname of Bog Man Bos because of all the bad novice chasers he's had to ride lately, many of whom dump him in the mud.

After racing I went to John Skull's surgery for treatment, then met Carl, Fluffy and Charlie Morlock, Nicky Henderson's assistant, to go to Lorna Vincent's party at nearby Great Shefford. There was a good turn-out of lady jockeys, including Penny Ffitch-Heyes and Candy Moore, who is to marry Billy Morris in the summer.

Sunday 21 February

After last night's party a lie-in was called for, but I didn't enjoy it very much because I was dreading a photo session due to start at the house at 10.00 am. These things usually take ages and can be very tedious, but today two easy-going chaps had the whole thing over and done with in three hours, which may seem a long time but is quite short by normal photo session standards. It meant I was able to enjoy Sunday lunch at the Maytime in Astral with Carl, Woody and Carol, and Bob and Helen Kington. Afterwards we went back to Woody's house for a quiet afternoon watching videos.

My collar-bone feels great, but life seems to have slowed down quite a bit since the injury, and I wonder how difficult it will be to get back into the jockey's normal routine of riding out and dashing to the races every day.

Monday 22 February

The film crew from TVS, which should have started following me today, has postponed everything for a week in the hope that I will be back riding by then. I hope so too: I'm really missing racing and I have reached the stage where I don't even like looking through the runners in the *Sporting Life* each morning. I saw John Skull again today and he told me that all is going well and that I should be back in action within a couple of weeks. I just hope he's right.

Tuesday 23 February

I would never begrudge anyone a winner, but it does hurt when you see someone else succeed on a horse that you would normally have been riding yourself. So I have to confess that I wasn't too upset when none of the three good rides I would have had at Huntingdon today won, although Polar Sunset finished second under Carl. Captain Forster was going to retire Polar Sunset after today, because the horse has not seemed his usual self lately, but he ran so well that it has been decided to give him a further lease of racing life, and I hope I will be able to ride him next time out. Fluffy fell in the novice chase, but emerged unscathed.

Today was one of those rare occasions when I drove all the way there and back myself instead of snoozing in the passenger seat. However, Dad continuously criticised my driving throughout both journeys – next time he can flipping well drive himself!

Wednesday 24 February

First thing this morning I had a preliminary meeting at Radio Oxford about a programme I'm going to record for them in a few weeks' time. It's rather like *Desert Island Discs*, and I have to choose eight of my favourite records.

Later in the morning I was driven to London to Austin Reed of Regent Street for a fitting. Austin Reed very kindly kit out the British jump jockeys' team for their travels abroad during the summer, and this year I've been asked to join the squad. I met Mr Tony Schooling, the store director, and was measured for my team 'uniform'. Austin Reed were very generous and also gave me a suit of my own choice and a couple of jumpers. I normally wear cords and a sweater to the races, so the jumpers will certainly help.

I slept all the way home, as usual, then had a haircut in Newbury and went to John Skull for more treatment.

Thursday 25 February

Although I wasn't personally involved, today turned out to be similar to that day at Ascot a fortnight ago, starting full of anticipation and ending on a very sad note.

A superb card at Wincanton saw the return to action of two of jump racing's superstars, Burrough Hill Lad and See You Then. Burrough Hill Lad had been off the course for two years for a variety of reasons while See You Then, partnered today by Steve Smith Eccles, was due to bid for a record fourth successive Champion Hurdle at Cheltenham next month, not having seen action since the Cheltenham race last year.

Although Richard Rowe on Burrough Hill Lad ran well enough to finish a distant but satisfactory third in the three-mile chase, See You Then's comeback was a complete disaster. He broke down just before the second last hurdle with a major problem in his off hind leg. Strangely, all his previous problems have been confined to his forelegs. He will survive, but he won't race again, and it is always sad to see a true champion finish his career in this way. Nonetheless he will go down as one of the great hurdlers of all time.

To make matters worse, our stable had problems of its own. None of our four runners ran well, and poor Brown Gambler had to be put down after cutting through his tendon at the water jump. I was very upset, and so was Annie, who looked after him in the yard.

To cap what was generally a sobering day for jump racing, Richard Guest recorded his eighth fall in five days. That is one record that neither I nor any other jockey will be trying to beat.

Monday 29 February

After three very dull and boring days, spent mainly in John Skull's treatment room, it was a relief to have something positive to do today when the TVS crew arrived to begin their week's filming. They started by filming me doing office work and they also interviewed me. In the finished film the interviewer's questions won't be heard, only my answers, so I had reply in a way that did not make it sound like a question-and-answer session, which proved quite difficult.

I'll be fit to ride again by Wednesday, and the crew will be filming me at two race meetings.

March

Tuesday 1 March

I had to make a very early start this morning in order to get to Newmarket by 7.30 am to be filmed riding work on Gee-A in preparation for Cheltenham, which begins a fortnight today. Unfortunately the ground was too hard for the schooling fences to be used so we had to make do with the all-weather gallop.

We bought some Newmarket sausages and stopped for breakfast before returning home. I spent the afternoon being filmed running on the downs with Chris Maude. It was extremely cold.

Wednesday 2 March

Today's the big day! I was due back in the saddle for the first time on a racecourse since the fall, partnering Regal Nod at Worcester, but first I had to go to the Jockey Club headquarters in Portman Square in London to see Dr Michael Allen, who is the only person who can pass me fit to ride again.

I didn't feel 100 per cent, but I was nevertheless confident of passing. Dr Allen put two fingers on the break, and I had to pull his other hand towards me, then push away. Then I had to push it up to the ceiling and down to the floor. I managed this without too much difficulty, but Dr Allen was not happy because he could feel that the bone was still moving.

He sent me for an X-ray at a nearby hospital and as soon as I saw the results I realised I would have a job to pass. Sure enough, he explained that the bones had not reunited and that no callous had started to form either. I tried to convince him that it felt all right, but to no avail – he refused to sign me back on. He also told me to stop riding out or doing any other physical exercise that might interfere with the healing process. Finally, to my complete horror, he told me that he could not see me for another nine days.

So that was that. There was nothing for it but to find another jockey to ride Regal Nod – Martin Bosley took the mount – and to contact the film crew to tell them not to bother going to Worcester. At the end of a bitterly disappointing day it was decided that the crew will call a halt until I'm fit to ride again.

Tuesday 8 March

Despite intensive treatment since my meeting with Dr Allen last week, it appears that the collar-bone is still not knitting together. So it has been decided that a bone specialist in Banbury, Mr Burrows, whom I have seen before, will operate today, taking a bone graft from my leg and placing a screw and plate on the break to hold it together.

I was due at the Horton Hospital in Banbury at 2.00 pm, but first I had to go to the Sheraton Skyline Hotel near Heathrow Airport to meet Shaun McMorn, a representative of Communications International, who are sponsoring me with a mobile 'phone which would normally sell for £1,800. What with a car, clothes and now a 'phone I've done pretty well lately.

I eventually arrived at the Horton at 3.00 pm, and was sent for a bath before going to the ward. But already I was having doubts. Even carrying a suitcase the collar-bone felt fine, and I was beginning to wonder whether I should have the operation at all. Nevertheless, I had my pre-med and was wheeled to the theatre, but as soon as Mr Burrows walked in I told him I felt much better. Perhaps he thought I was whipping round at the start, but he agreed to look at the bone and arranged for me to have an X-ray. Sure enough, it showed that the callous was forming at last, so the operation was cancelled and I was wheeled out again. I rang Carl and asked him to collect me at the end of an anti-climactic but encouraging day.

Wednesday 9 March

I had been due to record my Radio Oxford programme today but have already cancelled that and various other appointments as I had expected to be in hospital. Instead I went with Carl to Bangor-on-Dee, where he was riding today. This course, on the Welsh border, is one of the most rural jump racing venues. The nearest thing to a stand they have is a grass bank. Getting to and from it is one of the most difficult journeys on the jumping circuit, and we were home late.

Friday 11 March

A messy and disappointing day. I had to be at Sandown for 10.15 to see Dr Allen for a medical, then go back to John Skull's in Swindon for treatment, then return to Sandown to see someone else about the mobile 'phone sponsorship.

I was convinced I would pass the medical today, but I failed again, although Dr Allen is sure I'll be all right for the start of the Cheltenham Festival meeting next week.

It is doubly frustrating because Hywel Davies broke his collar-bone two weeks ago and was passed fit today, whereas I have now been side-lined for a month.

Saturday 12 March

After an uneventful day I had planned to have an early night when Jimmy Duggan rang to ask Carl and me to join him and his fiancée Wendy for a meal at the Peking Dynasty in Wantage. We met at the Yew Tree in Grove, together with jockey Luke Harvey and his girlfriend, and it was pretty obvious that the men were already well away. The result was an extremely lively meal as Luke became more and more out of order, eventually joining a table of drunk and overweight middle-aged couples. He was soon singing along with them, and had virtually taken over the entire restaurant before we finally got him away. Luke is a complete headcase but very likeable in his own special way. He particularly enjoys a good 'lads' night out', when he really excels himself.

Monday 14 March

Tomorrow sees the start of the three most important days in the Jump Racing Calendar, the Cheltenham National Hunt Festival. Many horses which have been trained specifically for this meeting will be put to the stiffest test this week, for the standard of runners in every race is extremely high. And I am sure that most of the jockeys, especially those who have fancied rides, will feel some form of nerves when they arrive at jump racing's headquarters tomorrow.

I am due to ride Prime Number in the Waterford Crystal Supreme Novices' Hurdle for Dad tomorrow, and Gee-A for Mr Hubbard in the Cathcart Chase on Thursday. I have mixed feelings about Cheltenham this year: the meeting has more atmosphere than any other jump meeting in the Calendar, and 12 months ago I was lucky enough to be in the thick of it when I rode a double on Gee-A in the Mildmay and The Ellier in the Kim Muir. Somehow I cannot see that happening this time. The first hurdle, however, will be passing the medical.

Tuesday 15 March

I bounded into the weighing room this morning full of hope and confidence, and happy to be taking part in such a great occasion, only to be stopped dead in my tracks by yet another failed medical. I was bitterly disappointed because I had felt I was certain to pass, and at that moment I wished I had had the operation. It would have been much easier if I'd known I wouldn't be fit, or even that I had only a slim chance of passing, because then my hopes would not have been raised at all. But Dr Allen had given me the impression that I would be all right, so the blow was doubly hard to take.

Carl took the ride on Prime Number in the opener and was going quite well until the horse weakened after the sixth. Peter Scudamore won the big race of the day, the Champion Hurdle, on Celtic Shot, beating the much-fancied Celtic Chief which was ridden by Woody. You don't often see Scu grinning from ear to ear, but that was exactly what he was doing as he came back into the winners' enclosure. The victory must also have been a tremendous boost for Celtic Shot's trainer Fred Winter, who is slowly recovering from a bad fall.

Dick Lovett Garages had a chalet in the tented village, which grows bigger every year and is referred to by many as the canvas city. This was one of the occasions on which I was due to go and meet some of their customers, not a very arduous task in return for a free car, but after the news from Dr Allen I felt really low and not at all like socialising. Still, it had to be done, and in the end it went well.

I have to see Dr Allen again on Thursday morning before riding Gee-A in the Cathcart. I won on him here last year, of course, and the thought of riding him round Cheltenham again at the Festival meeting is really exciting.

Wednesday 16 March

I did not have a ride at Cheltenham today anyway, so I felt full of Festival spirit right from the start, and enjoyed my lunch in Dick Lovett's chalet. An excellent afternoon's racing was highlighted for me by Carl's win on Smart Tar in the Mildmay, his first ever Festival winner. Coincidentally, I won the same race on Gee-A last year. It was also a good day for the Sherwood brothers, trainer Oliver and jockey Simon, who landed a 55–1 double in the two Sun Alliance races, while Pearlyman demonstrated that he is still the best two-mile chaser in training by beating Desert Orchid and Very Promising in the Queen Mother Champion Chase.

Our own celebrations of Carl's win began on the course, which we did not leave until two hours after the last race. We stopped for supper at the Pound in Goosey, by which time Luke Harvey, always a front runner when it comes to celebrating something, was already well away. Because I am hoping to ride tomorrow, I made sure I got home early.

Thursday 17 March

I was very nervous this morning, terrified of being turned down again, and I tried not to think about the racing. But in the end I went through the form in the *Sporting Life* and came to the conclusion that Gee-A had a really good chance. I was really buzzing on the way to the course, but by the time I met Dr Allen I was shaking.

I failed again.

This was the fifth time and I just could not believe it, and neither could the other jockeys. In silent disbelief I took my colours back to the men's changing room and took my saddle back from my valet John Buckingham. Then I went back to the ladies' changing room in a state of shock. I had missed a good Festival ride in what was also Gee-A's Grand National prep race, and the disappointment was overwhelming.

I would have gone straight home there and then, but once I had recovered sufficiently I had to do my stint in Dick Lovett's chalet, and I also wanted to see Fluffy riding Accarine in the Foxhunters' Chase. Because of my mood I found it hard to be sociable with Dick Lovett's customers, but I did my best. In the meantime Fluffy started favourite in the Foxhunters' but could finish only third. Robbie Supple took the mount on Gee-A and although he ran well and stayed on, he was beaten 15 lengths by Brendan Powell on Private Views.

However, the day was brightened considerably by Woody's tremendous double on Kribensis in the Triumph Hurdle and Charter Party in the Gold Cup, and I was really pleased for him. Unfortunately Carol had been laid low by a tummy bug and could not be there, so instead of starting to celebrate on the course we went straight to Martin Bosley's parents' house in Bampton where everyone, me included, was in great spirits. We later learned that Carol had kept fairly cool watching on television as Woody won the Triumph, but when he won the Gold Cup as well she could not contain herself any longer, and ran out into the street whooping with delight, much to the amazement of passers-by!

And so another great Festival meeting came to an end. For me personally the whole thing was a complete anti-climax, but you cannot fail to become caught up in the wonderful atmosphere of Cheltenham, and I was also really pleased that Carl and Woody had done so well. One rather ominous note was sounded however. The two top Flat race trainers, Guy Harwood and Michael Stoute, came to Cheltenham with just one runner each, and both horses won easily. I wonder what would happen if they decided to go in for jump racing in a big way?

Saturday 19 March

This evening a large group of us gathered in the Liaison
restaurant in Oxford for more Gold Cup celebrations.
These included Jimmy Duggan and Wendy, Mark
Richards and girlfriend Julie, Bob and Helen Kington,
Guy Roberts, Neil Morrice of the *Racing Post*, Luke
Harvey and girlfriend Alison, Martin and Sarah, Carl and
myself and, of course, our hosts Woody and Carol.

You may have noticed that Fluffy's name is missing
from that list – he was invited, and his absence is
something he was unable to explain either satisfactorily
or convincingly. Fluffy was dating a girl for the first time
tonight, and rang me to ask where we were all meeting.
I told him the Liaison in Oxford, but instead he ended up
in the Peking Dynasty in Wantage, having an intimate
candle-lit dinner for two! He later claimed that he didn't
know where we were, and of course I stuck to my
guns and explained that I had given him perfectly clear
instructions. The fact that he went to the wrong place
when he was dating a girl for the first time cannot be put
down to mere coincidence. . .

At the Liaison Woody called for champagne. He
looked exhausted, but was determined to enjoy himself,
and the party got more and more noisy. The wine
flowed and it finally became silly: needless to say the
people responsible were Messrs Bosley, Harvey and
Llewellyn. We played a particularly daft game in which
you place a spoon on the rim of a champagne bottle, and
the contestant has to pick it up with his mouth while
standing on one leg, holding the other leg in the opposite
hand next to the opposite ear. Quite a few managed this.
The spoon was then placed on the rim of a Coke bottle,
and there were a lot of fallers here, leaving only Carl,
Mark and Martin in the running. Mark fell at the next,
a tonic bottle, which left Carl and Martin to contest the
finish over a vase and a miniature milk jug. However,
they both fell at the last, and the race was declared void.

Numerous other ridiculous games followed until we
finally called it a day at 3.00 am. Being a non-drinker I

was able to sit back and view people's antics with great amusement. Gold Cup victories are very special, and we'll remember this evening for a long time.

Monday 21 March

I woke up with a tremendous sense of relief this morning. Yesterday I drove to Dr Allen's house and was passed fit at last! Now I can begin to concentrate on getting back into shape with a fitness campaign of running, swimming, squash and riding out as much as possible before the National, which is now just under three weeks away.

This evening Carl and I went to Liverpool for the Aintree Press Dinner. It was a very enjoyable occasion. Ginger McCain, who trained the great Red Rum, made an amusing speech, and I met John Hughes, Clerk of the Course at Aintree, and Ivan Straker, Chairman of Seagram, who sponsor the National and who have been largely responsible for keeping it going. A question-and-answer session followed the dinner, and after that I had several interviews. In the meantime Carl had spoken to Ginger McCain and picked up the ride on Kumbi in the National, so he was pleased he'd made the trip.

Tuesday 22 March

We stayed overnight in Liverpool and this morning walked the National course, where most of the fences were still being constructed. They look quite formidable when you stand by them, but if your horse is good enough it gives you the confidence not to be overawed by them. I will have the added advantage of having ridden the National course before, when I came fourth in the 1986 Foxhunters' Chase on Gala Prince. I arrived home in time for evening stables, followed by a game of squash and a swim.

Friday 25 March

My first ride back today was not a particularly
distinguished one. I rode Belinda Vard in the novice
hurdle at Newbury, and had to pull up before the second
last. She had run well for me at Cheltenham on New
Year's Day, but was very much in season today and
never went well. I felt sick and dizzy afterwards, partly
because it was my first race ride for such a long time but
partly because I think that on top of everything else I'm
developing 'flu. I had to give up my ride on Merryett
in the next: Martin Bosley substituted and the horse ran
well to finish sixth.

Although I felt rough, I went straight from the
racecourse to record my interview at Radio Oxford,
which finished at 7.30.

Saturday 26 March

I had two booked rides at Newbury today, but I felt
unwell and had to give them up. First the weather, then
the collar-bone, now the 'flu! When will it all end? In the
event, both horses finished second, so at least I didn't
miss a winner.

I decided to take the weekend off, and Carl and I went
to stay with his parents in Pembroke, where they have
a gorgeous farm. It was good to have a break, but life is
never simple. The central locking system on my car is
playing up and the only thing that opens is the boot, so
Carl and I are having to climb in and out of the windows
à la Dukes of Hazzard.

Monday 28 March

I felt much better today and was fit enough to ride Sir Kenwin at Hereford. We were unplaced but he gave me a great ride. I took Dad and Peter Cundell with me – one door of the car is now unlocked, which is just as well: I can't imagine Mr Cundell squeezing himself through the window!

Tuesday 29 March

The fact that I am a girl riding in the National is kindling much press interest, and the interviews are beginning to pile up. Next Wednesday I'm on *Wogan,* which I'm really dreading as it's a live show in front of a studio audience. Today I had an interview with the *Sunday Mirror* at Sandown, and as my car is being serviced I hitched a lift there with Hywel Davies. I'd asked Hywel because he can normally be relied upon to leave the course promptly after racing, and I needed to be back early to collect my car, which was being delivered to the house. Today, however, Hywel lingered, I was late back, the man from the garage suffered a sense of humour failure and took the car back to Swindon, and I had to flog in there to collect it.

Thursday 31 March

I went to London this morning to do a studio session for some fashion photographs that will appear in the *Sun* around Grand National time. My uncle Reg, who I call 'Waggy' and who is a brilliant uncle, came with me as he had business in London.

I arrived at the studio at 9.30 and it took three-quarters of an hour to be made up – I didn't think I looked that bad! Next, I was shown the outfits that I was to wear, slinky little mini-skirts and suits that weren't my style at all, although the woman in charge seemed to think they were just right. The photographer began to take numerous shots of me, standing or sitting on a huge sheet of white paper that formed both the floor and the background.

Halfway through the session Waggy appeared, and for some reason – probably because I looked and felt so out of place – his presence sent me into an enormous fit of giggles from which I just couldn't recover. Tears of laughter streaked my carefully-applied make-up, and the people doing the session were clearly stunned. I suppose they had never seen anything like this before. Anyway, Waggy was sent out before he could cause any more chaos, and I popped out for a while to feed the meter and to try to calm down, before finally finishing the session at 1.30 pm.

When we got home there was a film crew from BBC North West waiting to film me at my training exercises as part of a programme they are doing for the National. I started with a four-mile run, then played 40 minutes of squash, finishing with 50 lengths (1,000 metres) of Wantage swimming pool. After five lengths the film crew appeared to have all the footage they needed, and stopped for coffee while I plugged on. I did my 50 lengths and got out, only to be told to do three more lengths so that they could get various camera angles. They also filmed me riding my old showjumping pony, Ballan, bareback over a few bales of straw, before finally leaving at 7.00 pm. They'll be back tomorrow though. What a day!

April

Friday 1 April

The BBC crew were here again this morning, filming
me riding out and working in the yard. Then the *Daily
Mail* arrived to take photographs, followed by some
people from a new magazine called *Hello*. I seem to have been
inundated by the media recently as part of the National
build-up, and I'm looking forward to having some time
on my own.

I'm also looking forward to going racing tomorrow to
ride Nodalotte in the two-mile novice chase at Southwell,
near Nottingham. As it is Easter weekend there are
plenty of meetings and rides to choose from – I also had
the opportunity of riding Roving Glen at Towcester
tomorrow or Just Acquitted at Uttoxeter. Just Acquitted
was only narrowly beaten at Newbury last time out and
is a tempting ride, but Nodalotte is my choice, partly
because he's already won twice for me this season.

Saturday 2 April

For a while this afternoon I thought I might have missed
a winner. Nodalotte's race wasn't run to suit him; it was

too fast and I think he needs an extra half-mile on the firmer ground. Meanwhile, I knew that Roving Glen and Just Acquitted had both started favourites, Just Acquitted at 4–6.

I stopped at a bookie's on the way home to find out how they had fared, but the shop wasn't covering either meeting. Eventually I contacted Rod Simpson's wife Eileen on the carphone and asked her to check the results on Ceefax. Neither horse won, and I have to confess I was relieved. It may be a terrible way of thinking, but we're all human and nobody likes to miss a winner.

In the evening Chris Nash had a party to celebrate the fact that he, Carol and Luke Harvey all had birthdays in the same week. I had arranged to go with Carl and Luke, and by 9.30 I was becoming impatient. I knew that Luke had ridden a winner at Towcester, and I assumed they had stopped for a few celebratory drinks on the way home, although I thought they might have done the decent thing and collected me first!

However, by 9.45 I discovered that my suspicions were totally false. They were at Northampton General Hospital – Carl had had a bad fall in the last. He has pulled the ligaments between both arms and shoulders, which is apparently the equivalent of dislocating your shoulder and not to be recommended, and is in considerable pain. So he and I never made the party. Luke did, though, and I'm told he was characteristically very badly behaved.

Sunday 3 April

Two more interviews this morning. Carl can't move, and has told Ginger McCain that he is very doubtful for the National, although Mr McCain is kindly keeping the ride open for him.

I spent a lot of time at the Wantage sports centre; swimming, training and playing squash. At the end of the day I treated myself to a sunbed. The pressure for the National will really build up this week, and this was probably my last chance to relax until the race is run.

Monday 4 April

Easter Monday is the busiest day in the National Hunt Calendar, with 12 meetings up and down the country from Carlisle to Newton Abbot. However, my choice of meeting was made for me: Dad wanted me to ride Prime Number at Chepstow. He is owned by Ken Knox and Barry Wilsden, two of the very best owners one could wish for.

Sadly, Prime Number pulled up after the third, and we still haven't discovered what was wrong. He felt awful going to the hurdle, and I pulled him up as soon as we'd jumped it because I thought he had gone lame. But then he began to jog on again and appeared sound, which was a great mystery.

Naturally, the owners were very disappointed, and could not understand why I had pulled him up when he appeared sound back in the unsaddling area. Fortunately, the vet had been by the hurdle and had seen what happened, and he told me I'd done the right thing. He said he would back me up if there was any trouble from the stewards, and he also spoke to the owners.

I picked up a spare ride today on Young Nicholas, trained by John Roberts at Taunton. He hadn't run well for ages but went much better today, finishing fourth.

Tuesday 5 April

After an interview with ITN at the yard at 8.30, I left for Uttoxeter with Woody, Brendan Powell and Martin Bosley. Brendan's own car has been stolen, and it contained quite a few valuable items, including his passport.

I was riding Celtic Fleet for Mr Spearing in the three-mile-two-furlong novice chase. This was only his second run over fences, and the ground was very heavy, but he jumped like a stag and gave me a great ride,

finishing fifth. The horse has had four operations for
wind problems, and the vet says he can't have any more,
but on today's form he must surely go on to win a novice
chase before too long.

On the way home I competed with Woody and
Brendan to see which of us received the most calls on
the carphone. Normally I wouldn't have many, but as
the National approaches they're flooding in, and I think
I won by a short head today. Went to bed with the
sobering thought that tomorrow is *Wogan* – I'm dreading
it more than ever.

Wednesday 6 April

Wogan day! My worst fear! My most terrifying day!

I had no rides today but I went to Ascot anyway
so that Richard Pitman, whom I adore, could interview
me about girls riding in the National. I'm not normally
nervous about these sort of interviews, but today the
Wogan butterflies were already starting to get to me.

Fluffy had gone on with Dad, and I took my own
car, having arranged to meet Uncle Waggy and my
great pal Tina Cassan, known as 'Bism', at the course.
Bism is an irreplaceable friend – we have known each
other since our schooldays – and a great one for 'girly'
chats. She and Waggy were there to hold my hand and
take me up to London. This was where the trouble
started.

I do not have the world's greatest memory, and when
Fluffy collected my car keys from me to drive back to
East Ilsley I had already forgotten that all my newly
cleaned and pressed *Wogan* clothes were in the boot. It
was only when Uncle Waggy and Bism arrived that I
realised what I had done. Consequently, our planned
leisurely journey to London turned into a wild chase back
to the village, and it was pure luck that Fluffy had gone
straight home and had not stopped anywhere on the way.
By the time I arrived for make-up at the BBC studios my
hands were shaking and my mouth was dry.

Also appearing on the show was Allison Fisher, Britain's best woman snooker player, so I thought that at least someone else was probably feeling as nervous as I was. But Allison seemed to ooze confidence as she played trick shots with Terry Wogan, almost taking the interview to him. Meanwhile, I waited nervously in the wings.

In the event, the live interview was much less of an ordeal than I had envisaged. To start with, I did not have to walk on when Terry Wogan announced me: I was already seated and he came over to me. I had been worried about facing a live audience, but because of the strong lights directed at the stage I could not see them anyway, so I began to feel relaxed.

Terry's introduction was quite flattering, and it ended in my giving him the answer to the question he had asked me earlier, 'Do you think 40–1 are good odds for you to win on Saturday?'. My reply was: 'Put your mortgage on it'. He then asked some fairly standard questions: 'How do men treat you at the races?' 'Are you afraid of injury?', and finally he said 'Do you think that being an attractive girl has helped you in your career?'. I thought I gave a pretty sharp reply: 'Well Terry', I said, as I touched his infamous knee, 'do you think that being handsome has helped your career?'

And that was it. All over, thank goodness, and now no doubt seven million people are stampeding to their local bookmakers to back Gee-A at 40–1 in the National. Help!

Thursday 7 April

I had a radio interview at 7.00 am, and although I'm not at my best at that time of the morning it seemed to go reasonably well. After riding out two lots I spent the next four hours in the yard being interviewed by *Today* newspaper and having my photograph taken in various outfits. If anything, it livened up the morning's work for the stable lads and lasses, who began to realise that I do after all have legs! I feel very out of place doing these fashion sessions, and I hope I don't have to do many more. Some pay quite well, though, and I can't afford to turn them down.

Today was the first day of the Aintree meeting. The atmosphere is really starting to come to the boil now, and I can't wait for the National on Saturday. Carl is beginning to think he might be fit to ride Kumbi and is having intensive treatment on his shoulder. Ginger McCain has kept the ride open, although to be honest I don't think there would be many jockeys queueing up to ride the horse. He has a reputation of not getting very high at his fences, and is generally a rather unsafe conveyance.

Friday 8 April

Soon all the interviews, photo sessions, training and fuss will be over – the real thing happens tomorrow.

I had one more interview today, with the *Daily Express*, before leaving for Liverpool with Carl, who'd had his final treatment and was clutching a handful of painkillers and praying he would pass his medical. We stopped on the way to watch the Foxhunters' Chase, in which Fluffy was riding the favourite Accarine. He ran well enough, but was never a danger to the surprise 50–1 winner, Newnham.

We arrived at the Prince of Wales Hotel in time for a meal and an early night. From my room I could hear the noise of the revellers in the bars and restaurants below, and they gradually became the cheers of the Aintree crowd as I drifted off to sleep.

Saturday 9 April

Grand National day at last! I made an early start, and was at the course by 7.00 am to meet Gee-A's connections. The horse looked in very good health and felt it, too, as I took him for a short hack up the inside of the course

in company with Clive Cox on Sacred Path, trained by
Oliver Sherwood and one of the most fancied horses in
the race. I felt very relaxed and not at all nervous as I
took Gee-A back to the stables and waited for Carl, who
was riding Kumbi for the first time. Most of the horses
were already out at exercise, a tradition unique to the
National, their jockeys and lads wearing brightly coloured
slip-on jackets with the horses' names on to make
identification easier for the punters and photographers
already gathered in numbers, even at this early hour.

I met Uncle Waggy at 9.00 and set off to walk the
National course with Carl, Penny Ffitch-Heyes and Bob
Champion, who was giving us plenty of advice and tips.
I already had a rough plan. I had decided to go down
the outside, because Gee-A doesn't like a lot of hassle
on the inner. I also wanted to get a good start and be
well up all the way, because he likes being in the action
without actually having to do the dirty work by leading.
I suppose the first fence is a danger: a lot of horses fall
there through going too fast. But I think the real problem
will be the third, which has a very big ditch in front of it.

Throughout the morning everyone involved in the
National was hounded by the press, radio and television.
It's all part of the Aintree atmosphere and ritual, but I
must admit it was a relief to have a brief respite from it
as I headed back to the hotel to shower and change out of
my riding clothes.

We returned to the course in good time for Carl to
have his medical. I was praying he would pass, because
I know what it's like to fail just before the big occasion.
Last year I hurt my knee in a fall on the Friday, and was
desperately disappointed when the doctor refused to pass
me fit to ride The Ellier in the National. Even if you
know you have little chance of passing, it doesn't actually
hit you until the doctor says no. Happily for Carl,
though, he passed.

I met Dad in the car park, and he gave me a special
elasticated breast girth and thick foam pad for Gee-A.
I gave this and the rest of my tack to my valet John
Buckingham, who won the race on Foinavon in 1967.
John checked it and put it all out ready for me to

weigh out later, and gave me Gee-A's green and white colours.

There were plenty of good luck messages pinned to the noticeboard in the ladies' changing room as I got ready with my fellow lady jocks Venetia Williams and Penny Ffitch-Heyes. I didn't envy Penny her ride on Hettinger, a notoriously bad jumper, but she was sponsored for charity at £100 a fence and was happy just to be taking part.

After one final television interview it was time to weigh out. I handed my tack to Ferdie Murphy, Mr Hubbard's assistant trainer, who told me to ride the horse as I liked and to enjoy myself. It may surprise you that such vague instructions should be given for a race like the National, but Ferdie's words were exactly what I wanted to hear. He has a knack of knowing how to get the best out of me.

Finally the call came for the Grand National jockeys to leave the weighing room for the paddock. Nervous smiles underlined the tense atmosphere and the crowds were already cheering as we paraded down the course in front of the stands before wheeling round and cantering up to the start. As there were 40 horses in the race the walk-round at the start was much longer than usual as all girths were checked, but at last we were called into line and brought under starter's orders. All the jockeys exchanged good lucks, and meant it, and then, to a roar from the vast crowd, the tapes went up and we were away.

The 1983 winning jockey Ben de Haan made the early running on Insure, but Gee-A had made the good start I wanted on the outside, and we were lying eighth as we approached the dangerous third fence. As Gee-A pinged it any doubt about him not jumping the stiff Aintree fences went right out of my head, and I knew that barring bad luck I was in for a great ride. Ironically Clive Cox, in whose company I had hacked up the course some eight hours earlier, had parted with the favourite, Sacred Path, at the first, and poor Penny Ffitch-Heyes' race came to a premature end at the same fence.

I had a good ride on the first circuit with Gee-A jumping very well, and as we headed out into the country for the second time we were just in front as

we jumped the 18th fence, with Tom Morgan on Little
Polveir and Peter Scudamore on Strands of Gold close
up. But any chance I might have had of finishing in the
frame disappeared at the 20th. Gee-A stood off a little
too far and jumped it slightly awkwardly. I misplaced
something in my back which severely restricted my
movement. The horse carried on gamely and jumped
Becher's immaculately for the second time, but I could
no longer give him any encouragement, and he would
soon be getting tired. After Becher's he began to lose his
place, and there was nothing for it but to call it a day.

It was a desperately disappointing way to end the race,
and I think that had I been able to continue we might
have been placed. But even so I had a marvellous ride,
probably the ride of my life, and the horse had at least
pulled up sound and well. All the jockeys returned in one
piece, although Carl hadn't done his shoulder much good
with a crashing fall at Becher's second time round.

Meanwhile, Brendan had won the race, and I was
delighted for him. Rhyme 'N' Reason had nearly gone
at Becher's on the first circuit, slipping back to last, but
Brendan had never given up and kept working on him,
and the pair had hauled in Chris Grant and Durham
Edition on the run in.

Eventually we got away from the course and on to
the motorway. We went to the Dragon Inn at Burford
to help Brendan celebrate. He was incredibly laid back
about the whole thing, and spent the evening drinking
endless bottles of Coke. To round off a perfect week for
him, his stolen car had been found, and one of his prizes
for winning the National was a brand new Citröen.

Despite my disappointment, it has been a wonderful day.

Sunday 10 April

The 'phone started ringing at 8.00 am, but I was already
away having treatment for my back, a trapped nerve
having been diagnosed. I was annoyed to read in many
of the Sunday newspapers that I had 'said' I would

have won if I hadn't hurt my back. That is a complete exaggeration and, I feel, irresponsible journalism. The public depend on the media to find out the inside sporting stories, but after my recent experiences I would advise people to take what they read in the papers with a pinch of salt. In all honesty, some of the stories are untrue. Naturally I was disappointed with the way my race had ended as I was having a tremendous ride on Gee-A, and if he had got the trip and carried on jumping the way he was, we might have finished in the first four. But no jockey with any sense would claim 'I would have won' when there were five fences left to jump, plus that long run in.

Monday 11 April

More treatment from Val Ridgeway, who tells me that the muscle causing the damage has been over-compensating for the collar-bone. I feel all right this evening, though, and should be fit to ride at Fontwell tomorrow.

Tuesday 12 April

From the noise and crowds and glamour of Aintree to rural Fontwell Park – quite a contrast! Each racecourse has its own atmosphere and Fontwell, with its figure-of-eight chase course, is a pleasant little track, well run, and usually attracts good crowds. Of course, places like Aintree, Cheltenham and Sandown, with their huge stands and vast expanses, have a real sense of occasion about them, but there's nothing wrong with Fontwell either. What can be very depressing is somewhere like Leicester, Nottingham or Wolverhampton on a wet Monday afternoon. I passed my medical, and rode Sir Kenwin for Dad in the three-and-a-half-mile chase. The ground was fast and the race wasn't run to suit my horse, and we finished last. I had no problems with my back, but Carl has been signed off for a few days as his fall in the National has aggravated his damaged shoulder.

It was decided after racing today that Sir Kenwin will not run again this year. He has been a good servant – I had three winners on him two seasons ago – and I hope he will be retired to a good hunting home. Believe it or not, I'm still leading the race for the lady jockeys' title, even though I've had only eight winners all season. We have all had a bad time compared to last term, but I am determined to be leading lady rider for the third year running.

Wednesday 13 April

I rode Roving Glen at Ascot today – alas, he pulled up. He's not himself at all at present and is a much better horse than today's run showed. Like Sir Kenwin, he will now be roughed off for the summer.

Dad is questioning my fitness, and it's hard to convince him that I'm OK. I think part of the problem is that some of his horses are not right and are running badly, and I'm pulling up quite a lot. But that's not because I'm lacking in stamina. I need a winner right now. I haven't had one since January, and it doesn't do your riding confidence any good to go so long without success. You start wondering what you're doing wrong, and trainers start wondering why you aren't riding winners. But I have two good rides for John Spearing at Taunton tomorrow, Bickerman and Scots Nogger, and my luck has to change sooner or later.

Thursday 14 April

In the event yet again both horses ran a little disappointingly. In the handicap hurdle Bickerman was upsides the eventual winner at the last, but weakened quickly on the run in to finish fourth. When he was a colt he was very naughty and difficult to saddle, but he is much quieter now he's been gelded, and I wonder if it wasn't just his cheekiness that was winning races for him last season. Scots Nogger was sixth in the handicap chase, and jumped rather sketchily.

In the evening a hire car arrived to take me to Manchester. Tomorrow I'm taking part in a television programme for Granada called *The Funny Side*, presented by Cheryl Baker. During the four-hour journey I caught up with my letter writing, and had an early night after a meal in my room at the Holiday Inn.

Friday 15 April

I met the other celebrities taking part in the programme, including the former Test cricketer Graeme Fowler and the swimmer Duncan Goodhew. We all had to play in a band – I played the piano – and we spent most of the day rehearsing and watching the other acts perform. We did it for real at 8.00 pm, and it went off very well. I spent a lot of time talking to Duncan Goodhew, who gave me plenty of advice about keeping fit.

Saturday 16 April

I rode Merryett at Stratford today, but as I expected the track was too sharp for her and we could finish only fifth. We visited McDonald's on the way home.

Being smaller than most of my male colleagues, I do not struggle to do light weights. Whenever I go out for a meal, I invariably order a small salad, then steal everyone else's chips and whatever else I can lay my hands on when I'm not being watched! I therefore feel a little sorry for jockeys like Fluffy, Woody and Martin, who have to watch their weight carefully, and spend hours in the sauna sweating off the excess pounds.

This makes it all the more amusing to stop at McDonald's. Martin and Woody will gorge themselves on calorie-filled burgers and french fries, washed down with a gallon of strawberry milkshake, which means even more time in the sauna for the lads. Race meetings at courses like Nottingham and Leicester used to be dreaded but are now rather popular. The reason is a new drive-in McDonald's just off the A46. I'm sure business is doubled on race days, as the dedicated professionals gallop to be first there on the way home. Once home, it's another race – to the sauna!

Sunday 17 April

Carl and I went to Huntingdon, where I had been asked to present the prizes in a charity clay pigeon shoot. I don't think that sport will ever become a hobby of mine, though.

Monday 18 April

I rode out for Mrs Bernice Cuthbert, who owns the Aston Park stud, on a gorgeous little horse called Goldfields. He's an ex-Flat horse, really cheeky and full of fun. I popped him over a few logs and will school him over hurdles on Wednesday.

Tuesday 19 April

No rides today, so after riding out I took the afternoon off and went to Oxford. I also made my holiday plans, arranging to go to Zante in Greece with a group of friends in June. There are about 15 on the trip, and Sarah Whitaker is organising everything. She is absolutely brilliant at this, and never seems to mind when people cry off at the last minute.

Wednesday 20 April

I schooled Goldfields at Henrietta Knight's first lot, and he jumped very well. I also had a sit on a horse called Chilworth Mandolin which Mrs Cuthbert has just bought. He was trained by Oliver Sherwood, but has lost his form lately, and we're hoping a change will do him good and bring back some of his early form.

I'm trying hard to get back to full fitness, and spent the afternoon at the sports centre playing squash and swimming.

Friday 22 April

Life has certainly slowed down since the National, but tomorrow is another big day – I'm riding Gee-A in the Whitbread Gold Cup at Sandown, the last big race of the jumping season. My main worry is the distance, three miles five furlongs. The National is different in that a two-and-a-half-mile horse is often suited to the four-and-a-half-mile trip, but over park fences I think that Gee-A is at his best over two and a half miles, and with Desert Orchid in the race the pace will be very fast.

Saturday 23 April

There was a huge crowd at Sandown today and they were treated to a very exciting Gold Cup finish, although unfortunately I wasn't involved in it.

Mr Hubbard had decided on new tactics for Gee-A to help him get the trip. The plan was that I was to drop him in a bit and, whatever happened, not to try to take on Desert Orchid. But in doing this Gee-A did not run well at all, and we finished a remote last. He seems to revel in being right up with the action and I don't think the tactics suited him. Also, he may not have quite recovered from his National run. Depending on how he comes out of this race he may be turned out now, or run abroad.

Desert Orchid under Simon Sherwood was an immensely popular winner, beating Kildimo and Strands of Gold, and the roar from the stands was probably the loudest I've heard on a racecourse.

We went home via the Liaison restaurant in Oxford with a good bunch of people, among them Carl, Woody, Carol, Martin and Sarah.

Sunday 24 April

I went to John Spearing's first thing to have a sit on Nodalotte, who was in cracking form, then on to Mr Mahon's to ride work on Just Acquitted. I was home in time for Sunday lunch and a lazy afternoon.

Thursday 28 April

An exciting day lay ahead at Hereford, with Nodalotte in the novice chase and Goldfields going over hurdles for the first time.

Goldfields disgraced himself. Because he is so brave when schooling at home I was looking forward to a good ride, but he completely bottled out and jumped disastrously, fading quickly three flights from home to finish second last. The one thing I thought he would do was jump! Don't horses make a real idiot out of you sometimes?

When you are walking back to the unsaddling enclosure after a horse has run an appalling race you are inclined to put together a speech to try to encourage the owners not to throw themselves off the roof of the stand in despair. You are also thinking of a line so that the trainer won't tell you that you'll never ride for him again. There are certain excuses in racing that have stood the test of time. For example: 'I think he needs further and a little bit more time' can translate into 'This horse is painfully slow and couldn't win a donkey derby, let alone a horse race'. Another old line is: 'Your horse is still a little green, and a little deliberate at some of the obstacles'. This often means: 'He's gutless and a complete rogue'. I hasten to add that these remarks cannot be attributed to Goldfields, whom I'd love to ride again in the future. Nor do I personally feel anything but the need to be honest with owners, 99 per cent of whom would prefer to hear the truth whatever it might be.

Nodalotte made up for that disappointment by running a cracking race on ground he does not really like to beat Giolming under Hywel Davies. We had a ding–dong battle from three out.

I had been desperate for a winner and it was a great feeling to be led back to the winners' enclosure again. John Spearing to the rescue once more! The stewards had both Hywel and me in after the race and spoke to us about excessive use of the whip, but it couldn't have been too bad because neither of us was fined or banned. Riding a winner again makes such a difference – it gives you more confidence. It certainly put the spring back into my step today as I walked back to the car when racing was over.

Hywel was none too pleased with me, adamant that I'd done him on the bend after the water, although he certainly got his own back at the next bend. Even when racing was finished we weren't the best of friends, so I was horrified to learn that he was coming home in the car with Luke Harvey and myself. But Luke is a master at defusing tense situations. He got into the car, winked at Hywel and said 'Well then, mate, outridden by a lady jockey again', and drove off laughing his head off. What a character! Nothing bothers Luke (except last orders).

Friday 29 April

I had one ride at Taunton this evening and arrived
there in good time, having driven down on my
own, a rare occurrence. But as I walked into the
weighing room I was told that the meeting had
been abandoned after the third race, due to slippery
ground caused by a heavy shower on very hard
going. Taunton is rather prone to this, and the
same meeting was abandoned for the same reason
last year. So I had a wasted trip, but one has to be
philosophical about such things in racing. I met up
with Tony Gorman, who came back in the car with
me.

May

Today was a Bank Holiday, so there were plenty of rides available. I opted to go to Ludlow, where I had three booked rides, and once there I picked up a spare in the first on a horse called Prince Tobique. Trained by Dai Williams, he was originally with John Spearing, and I had ridden him in those days. He hadn't run for ages but finished third today, which was encouraging.

I had the ride on Celtic Fleet in the novice chase because Peter Scudamore had been claimed by Martin Pipe to ride one of his. Peter and Martin have become the most formidable combination in racing. It was an exciting race, and despite one rather hairy moment we held on to win, Scu coming second. Scu is one of the strongest finishers in the business, and a quite brilliant horseman – we all admire him greatly. He is a nice guy who doesn't give lady jockeys any hassle. The person I would really like to beat in a close finish is Steve Smith Eccles, who is always rubbishing the lady jocks!

This was a better day – things are picking up at last. My other two horses, Scots Nogger and Kiri's Song, finished second and third respectively, so I went home feeling satisfied.

Wednesday 4 May

Yet another film crew descended on East Ilsley today, this time to make part of a programme about lady jockeys. Apparently it will star Jacqui Oliver, Lorna Vincent and myself, and they will even film Jacqui's wedding to Willy Hayes in July. The programme goes out later in the year, and I'm sure Steve Smith Eccles can't wait to see it!

I was filmed weight training and running. It was all a bit of a set-up really, because I had to use unfamiliar weights, and as I only ran about 50 yards I wasn't red in the face and blowing hard as I usually am after a run. I was also interviewed about various aspects of a lady jockey's life, but for some reason I don't think I came over too well.

There was one scene which I flatly refused to do. They wanted a shot of me going through the entries in the *Sporting Life*, and suggested filming it in the sunshine out on the lawn, with me relaxing in a deckchair holding a cooling drink. I explained that that was totally unrealistic, and that I would usually be at the kitchen table with a cup of coffee!

Thursday 5 May

A busy day with planners and surveyors in the yard. The place has become a bit dilapidated in recent years, and is not much fun to work in during the winter months, so my parents have agreed to sell it for building land and construct a modern yard next door.

I shall miss the old yard, and not just because of the horses. I've lived in this house all my life, and have very happy memories of the place. We brought up two fox cubs here, who lived until the age of 17, and we had a badger who used to come into the house to use the loo. Apparently badgers like to perform their bodily

functions in water, so the loo seemed the natural place.
We also had a donkey called Trots, who lived to be 33,
and a cow called Mrs Moo, which meant that we always
had plenty of fresh milk, cream and butter. I remember
having to beat the cream with an old wooden spatula to
make butter in the old-fashioned way in the days before
blenders and mixers. Dad used to milk Mrs Moo every
morning at 4.00 am, and would sometimes be greeted
by our neighbour, the trainer Kim Bailey, coming home
in his dinner jacket after a night out.

There were always lots of chickens clucking about, and
hundreds of baby ducklings in the spring. I shall be sad
when the bulldozers move in.

Friday 6 May

Life is more relaxed these days, with fewer horses to ride
out as the season draws to a close. I had a 'phone call this
morning from Corky, who is coming back from Ireland
next month to look for a job. I also found time to meet
up with an old schoolfriend, Grace Muir, for a shopping
expedition to Oxford. There are quite a few weddings
coming up this summer and I had intended to buy
something suitable to wear for them, instead of borrowing
clothes from friends as I usually do on smart occasions.
But in the end I bought yet another jumper and a
pair of jeans, and Grace and I had lunch in McDonald's.

Saturday 7 May

I drove a gang of local jockeys to Hereford today, where
I was to ride Nodalotte. Woody ruined the race for
everyone else by blazing a trail on Condicote Boy and
winning by a distance. Nodalotte was feeling the ground
so I just jumped him round to finish third. That was his
last race of the season, and he's going home for a while
to his owner, Mr Bowers, who has a farm near Tewkesbury.

How I wish all owners were like him and his family. Nodalotte has been my star horse this year, providing me with winners when I really needed them.

Everyone in the car was skint. Carl has just bought a house, Martin has just paid some big bills and Luke Harvey is always skint anyway. So we stopped at a chippy on the way home, and went to Luke's house to play Trivial Pursuit.

Sunday 8 May

Today was the final day of the Badminton Horse Trials, and I played my part in the Dick Lovett tent. I drove there with Carl and, when I wasn't needed by Lovett's, we walked the cross-country course with Bism and her boyfriend, jockey Jamie Osborne. The fences looked huge and I thought that of all the horses I ride only Nodalotte would take them on. I would like to have a bash at Badminton one day, but I think the dressage would drive me mad.

Carl has heard that he has been selected as a member of the British jump jockeys' team to tour Australia in June. He was picked because he won the conditional jockeys' championship, and is very much looking forward to it. Brendan is going too, as the National winner, along with Hywel Davies and Richard Rowe. I have been asked to join the team going to Belgium in July, which will be fun.

Monday 9 May

I made a very early start to the week – I had to leave at 4.30 am to be in Carlisle by 9.00. I was taking part in a children's television programme called *Get Fresh*, which is about the environment and encourages children to respect the countryside and its inhabitants. They had many animals and birds there, and I spent a lot of time

cuddling four baby owls – I adore birds. Whenever
someone finds a sick or injured bird in the village they
bring it to me.

I have a pet duck, Dickinza, a great friend who
never answers back. She came everywhere with me when
she was a baby, but unfortunately she has become too
big to be taken to pubs and restaurants any longer. I
had been asked to bring her with me, but I couldn't as she
is busy making nests at the moment and wouldn't like to be
disturbed.

Tuesday 10 May

I rode Goldfields for Mrs Cuthbert at the evening
meeting at Towcester. He has had wind problems, and
after his disappointing run at Hereford a few weeks ago,
when he ran much too free, I had planned to settle him
at the back near the outside. The race didn't go according
to plan, as sometimes happens, and we led until the
last, where we were badly hampered and almost brought
down. Nevertheless it was an encouraging run. On
the way home Carl, myself, Jamie, Bism and Dai Tegg
stopped for a meal at Browns in Oxford, where Dai
revealed his plans to spend the summer selling ice cream.
The things jockeys do in the close season!

Wednesday 11 May

Today I started my summer job, riding out for Paul
Cole at his yard at Whatcomb, just up the road from East
Ilsley. It is a lovely establishment with all its own gallops
and some very decent horses. Last year, doing the same
job, I fell for a colt called Insan, who ran really well. He's
usually still lying down, fast asleep, when I go into the
stable, and I have to sit on his back to wake him up. On
the whole I try not to become too attached to horses,
because riding them is simply my business. Sometimes,

though, it is impossible not to get a bit sentimental
about an animal and horses such as The Ellier, Gee-A
and Nodalotte will always have a special place in my
affections.

There was an evening meeting at Worcester, but I
didn't have a ride. The Jockey Club have arranged a number
of extra evening meetings to make up for those lost to
the bad weather earlier in the year. I don't altogether
like evening racing because they make for such a late
return home at night. It must be hell for the stable lads
who have a runner in the last and still have to get up early
the next morning. Being a stable lad is a tough job at the
best of times. They are never given nearly enough credit for
all the hard work that goes on behind the scenes.

Thursday 12 May

Amateur jockey Charlie Farrell brought Bajan Sunshine
up to Paul Cole's gallops this morning for a bit of work
as the horse is going for the Horse and Hound Cup at
Stratford on the final day of the season. In the afternoon
I did some shopping for my new house. Since Mum and
Dad separated three years ago, Dad has been living in a
cottage down the road, but he's moving to Yorkshire
in the summer so I'm taking over the cottage – and,
unfortunately, the mortgage too!

Now that I have the independence of my own home I
can look back on some of the amusing things that happened
when I still lived at Nelson House. I particularly
remember one occasion during the early days of my
relationship with Carl, when he stayed late one night.

Dad had a set routine in the morning: he fed the
horses at 5.15, came back to the house for a cup of tea
at 5.45, and was out again just after 6.00 to feed the
sheep. So the plan was for Carl to go as soon as Dad
left the kitchen for his sheep run. While creeping out
like a mouse, he tripped and crashed into the door. Then
he realised that his car was parked right under Mum's
bedroom window, so rather than risk waking her by

starting it up he decided to push it down the road a bit
first. Just as he was doing this Dad appeared on his way
to feed the sheep, and asked if he needed a tow!

Friday 13 May

There was a large crowd at Stratford-upon-Avon races,
probably because the Princess Royal was riding. She
doesn't expect any special favours when she is racing and
she shares the dressing room with us. She is completely
natural and on one occasion she kindly lent me a safety pin
to keep me decent. Considering all her official duties it
is amazing that she manages to keep so incredibly fit. I
took with me an Australian girl from Paul Cole's yard. Her
father trains in Australia, but she had never seen jump
racing in England.

I had the ride on Celtic Fleet in the novice chase, but
he seemed a totally different horse from the one that ran
at Ludlow ten days ago, hating the ground. He started
a well-backed favourite, and a lot of punters must have
been disappointed when I pulled him up after the first
circuit. He'll win again when the ground comes right.

Saturday 14 May

I went with Carl to the evening meeting at Warwick,
where I had one ride, Low Ration in the handicap hurdle.
She hadn't raced for a while and needed a run to prepare
her for her next race. We finished sixth. We were back
in time for a very late supper at Chris Nash's house,
where there was a good party in progress. Chris farms in
Kingston Lisle and has been a godsend to me on many
occasions, driving me to race meetings as far away as
Yarmouth and Hexham. I should be cooking for him!

Sunday 15 May

My day of rest was busier than yesterday. I went
with Carl to Newbury racecourse, where we had
lunch before the final of the Turfcall Stable Lads'
Quiz, for which I was to present the prizes. We sat
with the team from Stan Mellor's yard which turned
out to be the eventual winners, thanks in particular to
one lad who was a mine of useless information. The
prizes were good, holidays in France and so on.

We left the course at 4.00 pm, and once home I was
collected to be driven to Thame to record a programme
for the BBC called *Headliners*. This is very much like the
old *What's My Line?* programme, in which the panel
is given clues about a person's occupation and had to
guess what he or she did. In this show they had to guess
the person's identity, and they got me first go, which was
a bit of a downer!

Wednesday 18 May

After two very quiet days I went to Newton Abbot
to ride Scots Nogger in the two-mile seller. I'd been
begging John Spearing for ages to run him over two
miles, but as luck would have it we were nearly brought
down at the first and never got into the race after that.

Quite a lot of chat goes on between jockeys during
a race and some, such as Steve Smith Eccles, have
actually been known to tell jokes as they go round.
If a horse upsides you nearly falls, you might say to
the jockey 'Well sat!', or 'Bet you don't jump the next!',
or he might say 'I'm going to go any minute now!'. Or
if two jockeys are going round together on a couple of
tailed-off no-hopers one might say to the other 'Race you
to the line'.

After racing, all the jocks tried their hand at go-karting
on the track that the enterprising Newton Abbot
authorities have installed inside the racecourse. They

said it was impossible to flip a go-kart, although several
people tried hard. The stars were Simon Sherwood
and Steve Smith Eccles, who used carving-up tactics
that would have made even a London taxi driver
blanch!

Thursday 19 May

I rode Low Ration for Bill Perrin again, this time at
Huntingdon. I wasn't sure that she was 100 per cent at
the start, and although the starter passed her fit to run,
after a couple of hurdles I pulled her up lame. It was a
pity after her encouraging race at Warwick last Saturday.

Saturday 21 May

I went to the evening meeting at Warwick with Carl, although I had no rides myself. It was a pleasant evening, and
most of the wives and girlfriends were there. Carl won the
novice's handicap hurdle by a neck on the Mark Wilkinson-
trained Artesium, a very well-bred horse (out of Idle
Waters by Mill Reef). From there we should have gone to
a 21st birthday party, but instead, and I don't quite know
why, we ended up at the wedding reception of Captain
Forster's head lad's son. I expect there will be a few
people struggling to get up in the morning!

Sunday 22 May

Today I went to a cross-country event with Andrea Brown,
who was riding my old pony Ballan. It brought back
happy memories of the days when I rode him, although
our partnership almost never got off the ground. When
he first came to us he very nearly went straight back
again. Marcus was one of the first people to mount him,

and instead of doing what he was told Ballan jumped a five-foot gate, tore up Dad's newly-harrowed gallops and headed for the main road, at which point Marcus baled out. Miraculously he and Ballan survived.

Tuesday 24 May

I rode Scots Nogger and Mehooba at Ludlow. Scots Nogger finished second, but Mehooba, a very lazy horse, ended up tailed off. Like many horses she goes well at home, but fails to reproduce that form on the racecourse, although it has to be said that the ground today was very slippery.

Friday 27 May

A frustrating day – my two booked rides at Windsor were both withdrawn due to the state of the ground.

Sunday 29 May

I spent a thoroughly amusing and entertaining day at the Windsor three-day event, where I took part in a mini 'It's a Knockout' event in aid of the Princess Royal's charities.

There was an impressive line-up of celebrities: Janis Argyll, the world lady karate champion; Chris Bailleu, the Olympic oarsman; the television personality Keith Chegwin; Duncan Goodhew, the swimmer; Rachael Hunt and Mark Todd, the international three-day event riders; Alan Pascoe, who won the 400-metre hurdles at the 1974 Commonwealth Games; and a group of jump jockeys consisting of Peter Scudamore, Woody, Carl and me.

We all had to take part in relay races, through tunnels and up see-saws and so on with a dog as the baton!

The dogs were provided by the Barbour Dog Agility
Display Team, and were really excellent and well-trained.
Everyone taking part had an individual sponsor – I
was sponsored by Dick Lovett, and Woody by Charter
Party's owners. It was very successful, and a great
response from the spectators raised more than £2,000 for
the Princess's charities.

After the relay races the spectators were invited into
the ring to get the autographs of the celebrities in return
for a donation. We went round with a bucket, which
was filled with cash, including some notes. The overall
event sponsors were Beefeater Steakhouses, and I was
attacked by some 'Mr Men' dressed up as beefeaters.
They admitted to me that they do a lot of things
while safely disguised by their costumes that they would
not otherwise do! The Princess Royal presented Beefeater
vouchers as prizes at the end of a really enjoyable day.

Monday 30 May

Back to reality. I rode Goldfields and Chilworth Mandolin for Mrs Cuthbert at Hereford, where they both
ran stinking races and pulled up. Mrs Cuthbert is so
thorough in her training, and all her horses look and feel
so fit that there must have been a problem that will show
up in the next few days.

June

Wednesday 1 June

As there are only a few days to go before the end of
the jumping season things are very quiet, but amazingly
the media still seem interested in me. Today I had an
interview with the *Sunday People*, who were predictably
more interested in my social life than in my riding.

Thursday 2 June

The new BMW 5 series range was launched in Britain
today, and I went to the Bath branch of Dick Lovett
Garages to unveil the new car with the Radio 1 disc
jockey Simon Mayo. At the same time I was given
the keys to my own new car, as the first one
has already done over 17,000 miles. Due to some
administrative problem I could not actually take the new
one home, so I will collect it early next week.

    This evening I went to the Dargai Dinner in
Aldermaston. Dargai was a horse in training with us
for a long time, winning several races. He was owned
by a syndicate headed by Major John Urquhart, and the
connections have been meeting for an annual dinner in

In the weighing room at Cheltenham. (Gerry Cranham/Radio Times)

Sunbeam Talbot struggled round most of the Newbury course but could not make it over this ditch and unseated me. (Gerry Cranham)

Nodalotte, who gave me the first win of my professional career, made all the running at Taunton to bring us our second victory together. (Phil Smith)

Mum trained a winner, Cardinal's Outburst, with only her second runner and so gave me my first triumph of the 1988-89 season. (George Herringshaw/ Associated Sports Photography)

Geoff Hubbard, the owner of Gee-A, one of my favourite horses, accompanies me back to the enclosure. (George Selwyn)

ABOVE *Gee-A, my mount in the Grand National, loves being in the thick of the action.* (Roger Lings)

RIGHT *I find out just how big Becher's Brook really is before the Grand National, but we cleared it both times.* (Jack Kay/Daily Express)

OPPOSITE *Carl wasn't so lucky at Becher's. He had a crashing fall on the second circuit.* (Ed Byrne)

My brother Fluffy and I prepare to go into action on a day when neither of us had a broken collarbone.
(Gerry Cranham)

One of the happiest days of the year: Woody's wedding. He and Carol are flanked by ushers Corky (left) and Chris Nash (right).
(Bernard Parkin)

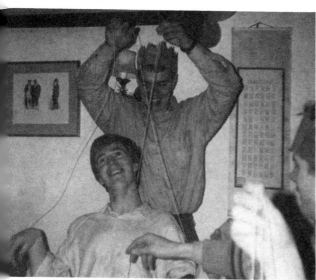

TOP LEFT *Martin Bosley, Woody's best man, makes a brilliant speech – even if he did embarrass me at the beginning.*

TOP RIGHT *Luke Harvey pirouettes in his best party dress.*

Martin pulls the strings to keep Carl under control.

I finished the season in June 1988 having won the leading lady jockey award, with ten winners, for the third consecutive time.

his honour for some years. I enjoyed tonight's dinner
– as always it was a good night. It makes a change now
and again to dress up and participate in the social side of
racing. It is fun to turn up and help out at sponsors' tents
and so forth, but I am at my most comfortable in jeans
and a sweater enjoying an informal evening out with a
few friends.

Saturday 4 June

I went to Stratford-upon-Avon for the last meeting of
the season. I had the pick of one or two horses for the
ladies' race, but I had opted for Mists of Time. Although
we started second favourite, the horse never got into
the race and we finished well down the field, which was
a shame since the crew making the film about lady
jockeys were there. Carl went to Market Rasen where he
fared rather better, winning the last two races to take his
season's total to 41 winners.

So that was it. End of season. End of term. Time to say
goodbye to some of the people who I won't see now until
the new season starts at the end of July. Time also to reflect.

When you look back on a year, you invariably wish
you had done just that little bit better, or that you had
made certain decisions which could have led to more
rides and more winners. Inevitably, my season had
its ups and downs, and I received an almost excessive
amount of publicity in the national press, the racing
press, and on radio and television. I had been hoping to
ride regularly for both Mr Hubbard and Mr Tinkler, but
in racing there are no guarantees and now I rarely ride for
either of them. My partnership with Darkorjon, albeit
a brief one, was a complete disaster. It meant that I lost
many winning rides for Colin Tinkler's syndicate, Full
Circle Thoroughbreds, which was a big disappointment.
I do hope they enjoy continued success, as the members
really love their racing.

It was Mr Hubbard who provided me with both the
high and the low points of my season. Gee-A gave me

an unforgettable ride in the National, and I would dearly love to ride him in that race again. He seemed to enjoy jumping the big fences, and so did I! However, I was very disappointed that I was unable to ride him at the Cheltenham Festival meeting, not just because I thought he had a good chance, but also because at that point of the season everything was going wrong, and I thought I was never going to pass my medical. Mr Hubbard brought over a young conditional jockey, Robbie Supple, to work for him, and he ended up riding the majority of Mr Hubbard's runners, which had an obvious effect on my fortunes. However, I still remain on good terms with Mr Hubbard, and hope to ride for him in the future.

On a brighter note, I finished the season as leading lady rider for the third year running, with ten winners, eight fewer than last year. This shows just how hard it is to secure good rides, and next season it will be even harder, because last season I was still an amateur until Christmas.

John Spearing was the trainer who always came to the rescue just when I needed a winner. All his horses seem to be so genuine, and 'jump for fun', especially Nodalotte, a bold, front-running chaser. 'Noddy' provided me with my first win as a professional on New Year's Eve, and also my first winner after my lengthy absence with the shoulder injury. If all horses jumped like him, National Hunt jockeys would spend a lot less time on the side-lines. Mr Spearing works very hard, and has some very sporting owners, so it is always especially rewarding to ride winners for him.

Every winner is special in its own way, but Silent Echo's victory at Warwick in December was a very moving experience. Gaining the race named after their son for the Blackmores made me feel proud for them, as losing Michael must have been absolutely devastating blow. Whether you are an amateur or a professional, money pales into insignificance when you see the pleasure you can give to people.

Although I had my own set-backs during the season, I'm now fit again and looking forward to my summer off, going on holiday and enjoying myself with friends. Some of my colleagues have not been so fortunate.

Venetia Williams, another lady jockey in the National, had a horrible fall at Hereford, breaking two bones in her neck. Even now it is not known if she will be able to ride again. On 14 May, riding Low Ration in the hurdle race at Warwick, I saw two jockeys lying on the ground as I jumped the last. One of them, Charlie Mann, seriously damaged his neck and will have to wear it in a brace all summer, while the other, the young conditional jockey Robert Bellamy, broke his thigh. Both may not ride again until 1989, and when I look at them, and at Venetia, I realise how lucky I am to be in one piece.

If my season in the saddle was adventurous, so it was off the racecourse, too. There were times when I seemed to be in the newspapers more often than the weather forecast, although I have never gone out of my way to attract this sort of publicity: it is the media who come to me, and I just try to be obliging. I began to gain the impression that some people were resentful of all the coverage, although I hope it hasn't changed me at all, and there were many times when I could have done without it, especially when preparing for the National. Dad summed it up when he told one press man: 'I wish you'd leave her alone and let her get on with being a bloody jockey!'.

So now I can relax for the summer and look forward to next season. I know it will be hard, but I am as determined as ever to ride winners. I'm very happy, surrounded by lovely friends and family. What more could anyone ask for?

Sunday 5 June

Sarah Whitaker's mother organised a local horse show, and some of the jockeys took part in the relay jumping. I shared Ballan with Andrea Brown, but we didn't do very well, and Lorna Vincent won the event. Luke Harvey did the commentating,

and was extremely rude about everyone taking
part.

Later on I took Carl over to Brendan Powell's house,
as Lorna was driving them both to Heathrow to catch the
Qantas flight to Melbourne for the British jump jockeys'
Australian tour. They are to spend a week in Melbourne
before moving on to Adelaide in South Australia. I
can't say that Carl seemed sorry that he wouldn't be
seeing me for a fortnight – he just couldn't wait to
go!

Tuesday 7 June
_____

Another Dick Lovett BMW 5 series launch took place
today, and this time I was able to take my own new car
home.

Wednesday 8 June
_____

Carl telephoned from Melbourne to report on
the first race of the series, which was held just
24 hours after they arrived. He wasn't placed,
but team captain Hywel Davies was just beaten
into second place, the official distance being half a
head.

Friday 10 June
_____

I went to Alan Hill's Bucking Bronco Barbeque, where
teams of jockeys took on the local hunt servants at
various sports and games. The jockeys, including Luke
and Martin, did not distinguish themselves, and the hunt
servants won.

Monday 13 June

Today I began a fortnight's holiday from Paul Cole's.
I will spend the first week just pottering about and
doing some shopping for my new house, and then next
Monday, when Carl gets back from Australia, we will
be flying off to Zante in Greece to join various other
local jockeys for a week in the sun. Among the gang
will be Woody, Martin, Jamie Osborne, Paul Croucher
and Tarnya Davies, and Nick Deacon, the *Sporting Life*'s
Lambourn correspondent.

Wednesday 15 June

Because I have to attend a Dick Lovett function at
Thruxton on Monday week, I need to get back from
Greece a day early. Jamie Osborne had agreed to swap
tickets with me, but today he telephoned from Zante to
say that security was very tight and that it would not be
possible. I'm extremely disappointed because it means
that I won't be able to go, and I won't have a proper
holiday this summer.

Monday 20 June

Carl and the rest of the team arrived back from Australia
this morning, but I didn't see much of him because he
flew straight off to Greece this afternoon! Brendan was
completely whacked from the 24-hour flight and said
he didn't want to see the inside of another aeroplane for
some time. Apparently they had a terrific time in
Australia. Carl's best placing was second in the final
race of the series in Adelaide, while Brendan and Richard
Rowe each rode a winner.

Sunday 26 June

The Zante gang arrived home today, minus Carl and
Fluffy who arrive tomorrow. I went to the Swan at
Shefford with Corky and Steve Taylor of the *Sporting
Life*. Corky wanted to meet Steve because he's looking
for a job in journalism. He has been writing Fluffy's
column in the *Newbury Weekly News* while Fluffy has
been on holiday, and has done a really good job.

Monday 27 June

An entertaining time at the Dick Lovett Porsche Advanced
Driving Day at Thruxton motor racing circuit in
Hampshire. We arrived at 8.45 am for coffee and a
briefing, and were then driven round the track by an
instructor in a Maestro. He went faster and faster, the
tyres shrieking, and it was quite frightening. After that
we each drove a Porsche around the circuit for three laps,
and to give a sense of competition he marked us out of
200 on the third lap. We were then let loose in Formula
Ford single seater racing cars. Next came karts, desert
racers and clay pigeon shooting. The competition among
the men was pretty fierce, and I presented the prizes at
the barbeque in the evening before leaving for Gatwick to
collect Carl and Fluffy.

Tuesday 28 June

After two weeks' holiday, which was rather an
anti-climax as the proper holiday never happened, I was
back riding out at Paul Cole's yard this morning. Things
will be pretty quiet now until I go racing in Belgium on 9
July.

July

Week ending Sunday 10 July

A fairly dull week, during which my routine consisted of riding out for Paul Cole in the mornings and organising the decorating and equipping of my new house in the afternoons. Hilde Purvis, my unpaid interior designer, who lives locally, is responsible for all the good things in my house and has tried hard to curb my excesses. I am delighted with the result. Her husband, Tom, works for BMW, my car sponsors, but this is a pure coincidence as I already have my car from Dick Lovett.

The week was made bearable by looking forward to my trip to Ostend at the weekend as part of a team of British jump jockeys riding in four races against the Belgians.

We assembled at Birmingham International Airport at 8.30 on the Saturday morning. The other jockeys were Richard Dunwoody, Peter Scudamore and Phil Tuck; and the three other members of the party were Julian Armfield, covering the trip for the *Sporting Life;* John Buckingham, our valet on a busman's holiday; and John Dorman, who organises the jockeys' trips abroad and who has also been helping me to write this book.

We were due to take off at 9.00 in a privately-hired seven-seater Piper Navajo Chieftain, but due to a problem locating the pilot we were not actually airborne until 9.30,

95

and this delay proved rather disastrous for certain members of the party. Because of our late take-off, we had missed our allocated 8,000 feet 'slot' and instead had to travel at half that height. The result was an hour's ride in what felt like an airborne bucking bronco, and Julian, one of the few not to feel ill, soon opened a book on who, as he put it, would be first to closely examine the inside of a strong paper bag. Scu started favourite at 3–1, but the eventual winner was Tucky, while Woody and John Dorman had turned yellow and white respectively.

Fortunately things calmed down after we crossed the Kent coastline and flew over the sea, so that everyone had more or less recovered when we touched down at Ostend Airport. We were met by Thierry Storme, President of the Hippodrome Wellington, as the Ostend racecourse is known, and driven to our hotel, a huge building right on the beach and directly opposite the racecourse. The bedrooms were the size of small aircraft hangars, each boasting two telephones, an enormous television set, acres of plush carpet and a balcony overlooking the sea. It wasn't long before various other members of the team were visiting my room, and I was quite flattered until I discovered that mine was the only room with a mini-bar, and I don't drink!

From the hotel we strolled across the road to the race-course, where we were entertained to a sumptuous lunch by the local racing authority. We then walked the course, guided by Philippe Caus, the Belgian captain, who has ridden in England for Josh Gifford and John Jenkins. Our own captain, Scu, rather let the side down by staying at the lunch table instead of joining us, on the grounds that he had ridden at Ostend on three previous occasions.

Interesting is probably the best word to describe the Hippodrome Wellington. There is a permanent chase course, but to create a hurdle course each set of hurdles is simply carried out in four sections by the staff and placed on the Flat course. The two-and-a-half-mile chase is run over a figure of eight, the horses going the 'wrong way' on the first circuit. Some of the fences would look more at home at Badminton, and there is also a white wall to be jumped.

July

The atmosphere at the course was very relaxed and easy-going. There were no gatemen, various people who seemed to have no official role wandered in and out of the weighing room, and apart from the first race going off as scheduled at 2.30, there did not appear to be much of a timetable. Three of our races were consecutive, which is pretty hectic in England, but here we seemed to have plenty of time to have a drink, watch the video of the previous race, and get ready for our next ride. There were eight races on the card, five on the Flat, two over hurdles and one chase.

There was no separate ladies' changing room and I shared a room with the apprentices who were riding on the Flat, but, unlike in England, we were able to wander in the men's changing room at any time, although we had to beware of a particularly amorous Belgian valet. It was a hot day, and I was grateful for the fridge, which incidentally dispensed beer as well as soft drinks.

Our first race was on the Flat, which I didn't enjoy very much because I just don't like riding in Flat races. The Belgian team were first and second in this, Scu and Tucky picking up the minor placings, which meant that our hosts led 18 points to 6. I was upset because my horse hit and killed a duck which had wandered on to the course.

We did much better in the first hurdle race, giving the opposition a complete whitewash. I led most of the way, but Scu passed me on the run in. Tucky was third and Woody fourth, and we now led 29 to 19. In the weighing room John Buckingham could not resist working, even though he was supposed to be on holiday, and was busy sorting out pads and weightcloths and tying caps. It was good to be able to sit with my team-mates between races, because I think you can learn a great deal just sitting in the weighing room talking to experienced jockeys. In England we girls can't do that.

Our third race, another hurdle, was even more memorable for me because my horse, Pol, backed down to even-money favourite, romped home an easy winner to give me my first victory on foreign soil. Tucky was second, and we had increased our lead to 46–26. Pol jumped really well, pinging through the hurdles.

The chase was an anti-climax for me personally. I was going pretty well on a horse called Zephyr, a stallion and a good jumper, when my saddle slipped and I had to pull up. Scu won the race from Philippe Caus to land a double, but in doing so his mount ran across Philippe's horse and took his ground, and Scu was soon in front of the stewards. The placings were reversed, but we had still won the match by 55 points to 41. Tucky picked up fourth place, which meant he scored points in all four races.

We were taken into one of the committee rooms for photographs and the presentation of individual silver-plated dishes along with a large and handsome team trophy which was quickly filled with champagne. Even better, there was a prize for the winning team of 80,000 Belgian francs, about £1,200. Much to Woody's relief we had agreed to split this equally four ways – he had drawn some bad horses and his own contribution to our win was two points!

Because of the fairly casual racing timetable, it was nearly 7.00 pm by the time we returned to the luxurious Therme Palace Hotel for a shower before meeting in the bar with the Belgian team, who were taking us all out to dinner. We went to a restaurant in the old town, whose proprietor also appeared to be the only waiter. As well as our party of about 15 there must have been another 30 people dining, so service was slow but, when it finally arrived, the food proved well worth waiting for.

After dinner our party split up. Scu, Woody and I went with the Belgian team to a disco called Griffins, while Julian, John, Buck and Tucky made a brief and unsuccessful visit to the local casino before returning to the hotel bar where they celebrated Buck's and Tucky's joint birthdays. Scu left the disco at about 2.00 am, but Woody and I and the Belgian team got a much longer trip, and it was 5.30 on Sunday morning by the time I finally crawled into bed.

I was woken at 10.00 am to be told we were leaving for the airport in 15 minutes. Fortunately, the flight home was much smoother, with drinks laid on as part of the service, complete with ice – Buck had filled our winning trophy with it at the airport.

Apart from being a successful trip it was also a very enjoyable one. There was a good team spirit, the Belgian jockeys could not have been nicer or more helpful and polite, and of course I rode a winner. I'm not sure if I would enjoy three weeks of touring Australia, but I will certainly have very happy memories of our excursion to Ostend.

Friday 15 July

Tomorrow is Woody's wedding day, and I feel absolutely terrible. I went to Carol's hen party last night and had a few drinks which, since I never normally touch the stuff, had an extremely adverse effect on me. Carol is apparently similarly afflicted, but then she had not arranged to play squash against Corky today.

Fortunately Corky was also feeling ill as a result of Woody's stag night. The game of squash was as competitive as ever, and the language as bad as usual, but it was interrupted at regular intervals as we were both feeling very dehydrated. It was a long 40 minutes, and both of us nearly passed out at the end.

At least I have a night to recover before the wedding, but the men, being gluttons for punishment, went to the Rat's Castle where they got completely blitzed.

Sunday 17 July

Yesterday was a superb day in every way bar the weather. I think that the average rainfall for July must have fallen on this one day, but it could do nothing to dampen the spirits of the wedding guests.

Despite their second run at a stag on Friday evening, reports had reached me that Woody, Martin and Corky, who had all spent the night at Woody's house, were in pretty good shape and raring to go. While Martin cooked a monumental breakfast, the bridegroom cracked open a bottle of vintage champagne and Corky, in his dressing gown, was out in the garden dancing to some very loud music. The neighbours were not impressed.

By the time we set off for the church it was raining heavily. Carl looked extremely smart in his tails, although he was wearing a rather stragely coloured cravat. It looked like a horrible orange blancmange, and he was reminded of the fact several times during the course of the day. As I proudly paraded in my own new outfit, all I got from him was 'I see you're going in your pyjamas'.

At the church the ushers, Chris Nash and Corky, looked like Tweedledum and Tweedledee in their identical morning suits, while James Davies and Tom McCourt, the three-year-old sons of Hywel and Graham respectively, looked absolutely gorgeous in their tails. They were remarkably well behaved, too. There were over 200 guests, some of whom had travelled a long way, as Woody's family hails from Northern Ireland. Distinguished guests from the racing world included Jonjo O'Neill, Captain Tim Forster, Peter Scudamore and David Gandolfo, who was positively bursting out of his morning suit! Fluffy was adjudged the best turned out, probably due to the fact that his set of tails were the only ones that did not have to be back in Oxford by 11.00 am on Monday.

Suddenly 'Here Comes the Bride' was thrashed out on the organ, and Carol approached the aisle on the arm of her father. She looked absolutely stunning: it was an emotional moment and I wondered who would be first to burst into tears. Before the start of the service we all sang 'Amazing Grace' rather badly, then the priest viewed the congregation and we were away. Woody and Carol remembered their lines, and amidst much emotion were pronounced man and wife.

It was still pouring with rain as we left the church, but no one seemed to care. Everyone was smiling, and the racing photographer Bernard Parkin was taking all the pictures. I was also snapping away, throwing confetti and getting very wet. The Dunwoodys and the Abrahams looked wonderful, and Corky raised a laugh when the ushers appeared to have their photograph taken with the newlyweds. He does have rather large ears, which made his top hat look rather comical!

The reception took place in a huge marquee erected on land in a small village called Ginge, outside Wantage. There was seating for nearly 300 people, as well as a sizeable dance floor. On a day of surprises, such as Martin and Woody arriving at the church on time, Hywel Davies stopping talking for two minutes and Lorna Vincent managing to fit into her dress, the biggest surprise of all was finding West Tip, on whom Woody won the 1986 Grand National, waiting to greet the couple as they arrived for the reception. It was a super gesture from trainer Michael Oliver.

After the formalities were over we sat down to a delicious lunch, which was interrupted halfway through by the arrival outside of Woody's 1988 Gold Cup winning mount, Charter Party. Everyone ate a lot, drank a lot and laughed a lot, and we still had the speeches from Carol's father, Woody and his best man Martin Bosley to look forward to.

A toastmaster was also employed, in the form of Richard 'The Human Sauna' Phillips. Richard has been around the Lambourn area for a number of years and is a great local character, to say the least. He is assistant trainer to Henry Candy and his impersonations of racing people are absolutely brilliant. But he is also one of life's great worriers, and sweats profusely on occasions such as this – hence his nickname. However, he got through the introductions well, slipped in an impression and made sure that the head fell off his toastmaster's gavel to raise yet more laughter.

The speeches were most amusing. Bob Abrahams went first, and spoke splendidly on what was obviously a very emotional occasion for him. Then Woody took centre stage and revelled in it. Not only was he entertaining, but he also took time to thank the many people who had helped him throughout his career, particularly Chris Nash's father Colin, who had given him so many opportunities as an amateur. Then it was time for Martin Bosley's speech, but was he in any condition to give one?

Due to the length of the earlier introductions, and
Charter Party's sudden appearance, the best man had by
now consumed a considerable quantity of wine. However,
he stood up, appeared to be reasonably steady on his feet,
and dived in head first. I nearly died when I heard his
opening line.

'Ladies and gentlemen, it is a great honour to be
Richard's best man today, but I must point out that I was
only the second choice. Gee Armytage was to be asked
but there were two factors against her. Firstly, she is of
the wrong sex, and secondly, she asked for too much
money.'

The marquee erupted in laughter – thanks a lot Martin!
The remainder of the speech was of the highest quality.
David Gandolfo was given a mention, not because he had
anything directly to do with the wedding, but because
Martin hoped he would give him some rides! Martin
also suggested that David Nicholson, Woody's guv'nor,
should refrain from schooling his horses on Sunday
mornings in future, as Woody now had a good reason to
stay in bed. 'The Fart' was now going at a good gallop.
To round off a quite brilliant speech he recited a poem,
an original idea which proved a great success. It ended:
'So here's to Richard and Carol, whose future's looking
rosy; wishing you the best of luck, from best man Martin
Bosley'. This was followed by prolonged applause, and
deservedly so.

It was nearly 7.00 pm and some of the guests began
to go home, but this beautiful day was far from finished.
Half of England had been invited to the party which was
to start at 9 o'clock. Many saw this as the chance to have
a breather but others headed straight for the pub. I'm sure
you can guess who they were.

By 10 o'clock the party was in full swing. The new
arrivals were beginning to get the feel of the occasion,
while the afternoon guests were coming nicely back
on the bridle, although one or two were beginning
to get tailed off, and were very soon to be pulled up. I
was still busy with my camera recording the evidence.
Martin, Carl and Fluffy were 'pulling double' over their
rivals and were definitely setting the handicapper a few

problems. Corky lost his camera, began to panic, found it, and started to creep back into the race. Luke Harvey was bombed out of his brain, which was nothing new, and Simon McNeill wasn't far behind him. As Woody and Carol prepared to leave for their hotel in Newbury, Corky announced that they were not going anywhere until he had played his tape of traditional Irish jigs and reels.

The dance floor was packed to capacity and everyone formed a huge circle, clapping and shouting. Woody and Carol were in the middle doing their bit to entertain everyone, then Martin and Sarah took over. We danced to well-known classic songs such as 'We're on the One Road, Maybe the Wrong Road', 'Paddle Your Own Canoe', and 'The Wife has got a Hairy Thing'. After these moments of madness, 200 people formed a human tunnel into which the newlyweds disappeared, emerging at the other end several minutes later, looking a little ruffled and sprinting for their car. The bride's bouquet ended up with Sarah – was Carol hinting at something?

But this was by no means the end of the celebrations: if anything it led to even more riotous scenes. The disc jockey played one or two slow songs to settle everyone down, and this gave some of the more amorous couples a chance to nibble each other without being noticed, or so they thought. Lionel Richie has a lot to answer for. But it was soon back to headbanging, and one or two people began to behave very strangely.

Michael Robinson, a young trainer and in fact Carol's boss, was diving head first on to the tables; not that silly, you may think, but you should know that the tables were full of bottles and glasses. Young Robinson was in danger of being gelded. Another popular activity was attempting to climb the 20-foot poles supporting the marquee, but no one was sober enough to make it to the top.

Finally the disc jockey played a few more slow numbers before packing up his equipment and hurrying to his car, no doubt relieved to be still in one piece. However, we did not want for music after that. As I mentioned earlier, Martin is just the sort of person you need on a Saturday night, and on this occasion he did not let us down. He went out into the pouring rain, got into his car, drove it into the marquee, and switched on the stereo. The party was on again.

But there is a limit to everyone's stamina, even that of National Hunt jockeys, and by 3.30 am I was busy ferrying people to their homes. My final trip was to collect Carl and Luke, always the last to leave, and always the noisiest. However, when I got back to the marquee it was deathly quiet and apparently deserted. I thought they had talked someone else into taking them home. I was about to leave when I saw a tablecloth move, and as I walked over to it I heard voices saying 'We are a table, we are a table'. I pulled off the cloth and there were Carl and Luke giggling like a pair of schoolboys and still insisting they were a table.

Time to go home. Good luck Woody and Carol. Who's next, I wonder?

Sunday 31 July

Carl and I were invited to Mark Wilkinson's owners' party today. Mark trains at Edgcote, near Banbury, in the yard where the late Edward Courage trained so many good horses, including Spanish Steps and Royal Relief. Carl rides regularly for him and rode Smart Tar to victory at this year's Cheltenham Festival. Woody and Carol were back from their honeymoon in Jersey, and we gave them a lift there.

It was a good day, marred by an incident on the way home. I was caught speeding, doing 46 mph in a 30 mph zone. I was livid, and to make matters worse, Carl treated the policeman as if he were some sort of god. 'Yes officer, no officer, thank you officer, cheerio then officer', as I sat there with a £24 fine and three points on my licence!

The new jumping season is now underway, and I'm anxious to find trainers to ride out for in the hope that it will lead to race rides. Now that Dad has moved to

July

Yorkshire, Mum has taken over the licence at East Ilsley, and of course I'll be riding for her when I can. But she won't be having many runners until the autumn and by then one can easily be forgotten. It doesn't look as though I will have many rides for Mr Hubbard, so I have decided to ride out for Terry Casey and Richard Mitchell.

Terry Casey is an excellent young trainer from Northern Ireland who has been training in England for four years with a good deal of success. Woody rides for him when he is available, but I hope to pick up some rides once the season is in full swing and Woody is claimed by David Nicholson.

Richard Mitchell trains in a village called Whitcombe in the West Country, and is currently building a magnificent new training complex. Nigel Coleman rides the majority of his horses, but as ever I'm always available!

August

Monday 1 August

I rode out for Paul Cole this morning, and although I'm keen to carry on doing so, I'll naturally be riding out for more National Hunt trainers as the jump horses start coming back into work.

Racing today is at Newton Abbot, and although I'm not riding the results will be scrutinised. I am longing for my first ride of the season, but at present there is nothing in the pipeline. However, August is always my quietest month, and it doesn't make me feel any less enthusiastic.

This afternoon I finally got round to moving all my belongings into my new house; a great relief, although I am also a little sad to be leaving Nelson House, where I've lived all my life. This means that Mum is now living on her own, but she does have half the canine population of Berkshire to keep her company, in the shape of her menagerie of terriers and whippets.

I have been asked to ride in Switzerland on 14 August, which sounds very exciting, even though details of the trip are still rather vague. Much as I like Market Rasen and Southwell at this time of year, a trip to Switzerland would be most welcome as I didn't manage to get away during the summer, apart from on the Ostend excursion.

Tuesday 2 August

Sadly, the Swiss trip is now off. That was quick! I was
told I could have ridden in only one race, and while
I would not hesitate to go to Carlisle or Hexham for a
spare, going all the way to Switzerland for a single ride
does seem to be stretching a point. However, there will
be another opportunity to ride there later in the year.

I schooled Roches Roost for Terry Casey this morning
as she runs on Saturday, and I will have the ride if
Woody is unavailable. Later, I tested Woody's fitness on
the squash court, and much to my annoyance he beat me.
I'm afraid that my language was not very ladylike.

Wednesday 3 August

While there is still no sign of my first ride of the season,
today's Devon and Exeter meeting resulted in two more
winners for the Martin Pipe/Peter Scudamore combination. At this time of the season they appear to be
invincible and tend to frighten off the opposition, which
makes rides even harder to find.

My afternoon was brightened by a visit from Jamie and
Bism, to whom I'm lending my bed. If it seems odd that I
should be lending them such a vital piece of furniture, I
should explain that I have been given a sponsored bed, which
measures 5 feet by 6 feet 6 inches. I've never heard of anyone
having a sponsored bed before, and I cannot imagine what
the sponsors expect me to do in such an enormous one!

Thursday 4 August

I left the house at 5.30 this morning to ride out at
Richard Mitchell's yard. Even at this time of the

day in August the roads are quite busy, mainly with
holidaymakers towing caravans which appear to be
bigger than my cottage and move at incredibly slow
speeds. I am not a very patient driver and as a result
I received several icy stares and uncomplimentary
hand signals from the tourists for overtaking at
points where they obviously felt I should not have
done.

The afternoon was memorable. I didn't have
a winner – I didn't even have a ride – but I did
beat R. Dunwoody at squash. Woody seemed to
be angrier at losing to me on the squash court
than he would be if I beat him in a photo finish.
He swore it would never happen again: come to
that he swore rather a lot this afternoon, which
must have constituted a severe dent to his male
pride!

Friday 5 August

A disappointing day. Although Roches Roost runs
tomorrow, I discovered that I am not required to ride it.
Also, Carl went to Market Rasen to ride Brave Hussar,
on whom he enjoyed much success last season, but sadly the
horse broke a leg approaching the seventh and had to be
put down.

Later, Carl and Corky, who had come down from
London for the weekend, came over to East Ilsley. Corky
managed to steer the conversation away from the topic of
racing, which was rather a good idea. The two of them
ended up discussing the prospect of buying a launderette
in Wantage and becoming business tycoons, as neither are
making any money out of racing at the moment. It was
very amusing listening to their plans to become the kings
of dry cleaning, but somehow I can't see those two as
budding yuppies!

Saturday 6 August

For the first time this summer the sun seemed to shine
all day. The ground up on the gallops was still good, and
Mum decided to school two horses over hurdles. She has
just acquired a lovely horse by Rymer. He stands 17.2
hands, and although a big horse he is very athletic and
schooled beautifully. He will probably be our first runner
of the season.

There was an evening meeting at Worcester, and
although I wasn't riding I went along with Carl, Woody
and Carol, Martin and Sarah and Corky. The weather
was glorious and there was some success for our team:
Woody got off the mark for the season on a novice chaser
that had failed to get round in two previous attempts,
but as usual he made it look very easy, and won by 30
lengths. Carl finished second in the selling hurdle and
Martin was fourth in the three-year-old hurdle on one of
his father's horses.

Passing through Burford on the way home we decided
to stop at the Dragon Inn, one of our regular haunts.
Very soon a highly entertaining discussion developed on
the subject of names, during which the male members
of the party were asked what name they would give to a
son they might have – not that any of them was in a fit
state to father a child at the time! Carl mentioned Lee as
a possibility, but was immediately shouted down. Corky
decided on Christy, as it sounds very Irish and, with a
name like that, the boy might turn out to be a jockey,
which Corky most definitely is not. We all decided that
Woody's son would be named Richard, which could be
appropriately shortened to Rich. Finally, Martin wanted
to name his son Winston Curtley in honour of two of
the West Indian fast bowlers who are currently wreaking
havoc among England's batsmen, but I don't think
Martin's father would be very pleased with that.

In Fluffy's absence I had to make a choice on his behalf.
I merely pointed out that he was still relieved that he had
not been christened Rupert, which was Mum and Dad's
original intention. Dad speaks with a soft 'r', and didn't

want his son to have to go through life being called
'Wupert'. A wise decision.

Sunday 7 August

I was up early to school Highbold for Mrs Cuthbert, as
he runs on Thursday. He is undoubtedly a character, and
I only hope he's in a good mood on race day – God help
us if he isn't! He schooled very well today, so maybe he
is beginning to settle down at last.

Trainer Rod Simpson gave a party this afternoon which
was bound to be entertaining. Flamboyant is the only way
to describe 'Rodders', and sure enough his party was a
lively affair. He doesn't do things by halves, so he hired
a complete rock 'n' roll band to provide the music.

Monday 8 August

I had an easy morning riding out for Mum, because
the majority of her horses are doing very little work at
present. She is renting a yard from Peter Cundell in
Compton until her new one is ready. It is beginning to
take shape and, when finished, it will be a lovely yard –
even nicer when it starts to send out winners.

I went shopping with Carl in Oxford this afternoon,
which normally would not present any problems.
However, as the weather is still very hot, Carl
insisted on wearing a pair of skintight pink and
black striped shorts which leave very little to the
imagination!

Tuesday 9 August

There was no racing today, which enabled the local
jump jockeys to take part in a jockeys' showjumping

competition at Finmere Show, near Bicester. It is always
an enjoyable afternoon, and we were made to feel very
welcome by the competition organiser Sally Haynes.
Sally is great company, and does not allow the fact
that she is confined to a wheelchair as a result of a bad
point-to-point fall prevent her from doing a magnificent
job.

The competition consisted of three sponsored teams
of five members. As I once harboured ambitions to be
an international showjumper, I was expected to perform
at a very high level, but in the event I was absolutely
useless and finished tailed off! The event was won by a
team consisting of Carl, Brendan Powell, Paul Croucher,
Richard Rowe and a certain R. Dunwoody, who one day
must surely get bored with winning – preferably on Terry
Casey's horses.

Thursday 11 August

At last I had a ride. The early morning drives to Richard
Mitchell's are about to start paying dividends as I was
given a ride on Biddable for him in a handicap hurdle at
Newton Abbot.

Although Biddable's form was very moderate, he had
worked well at home, and I was optimistic. However,
this proved a forlorn hope as the horse, after holding
a good position early on, dropped out of contention
four out and soon pulled himself up. This performance
finally exhausted the owner's patience, and Biddable will
be taken out of training. This is frustrating, because he
always works well at home, and the idea today was to
try a female jockey to see whether it would do the trick.
But it is expensive to keep a horse in training, and I can
understand the owner's decision.

As luck would have it, after waiting so long for a ride
I could have ridden at two meetings today. Highbold
was running at the Uttoxeter evening meeting, but I had
accepted the ride on Biddable several days earlier, and
I try not to go back on my word. My replacement was

John Webber's jockey George Mernagh, who was given an eventful ride. Highbold, after jumping the first hurdle, went absolutely flat out for two furlongs before pulling up before the last, completely exhausted. He can only improve on that – I hope.

Despite my disappointing ride, the return journey from the West Country was crazy to say the least. In the company of Simon McNeill, Carl and Crouch, who was giving us a lift home, we somehow got round to discussing choirboys. Carl claimed he used to be one and, to convince us of this unlikely fact, he suddenly burst into song, accompanying the car radio. I'm afraid Carl cannot even call himself tone deaf – the noise he made was dreadful, and it became even worse when Simon and Crouch joined in. Any other motorists witnessing these scenes probably thought we were celebrating something, when in fact between us we had not beaten a single horse all day!

Friday 12 August

I hope I never experience another day like today as long as I live.

Buoyed up by my first ride of the season, I set off at 6.20 am to school at Terry Casey's. Twenty minutes later, my car was lying in a ditch. Approaching a notoriously bad bend outside Wantage, I was horrified to see a lorry coming straight at me. I swerved to avoid head-on contact and hit a barrier which in turn sent me into the ditch. A very kind car driver stopped to help me, only for another car to crash into the back of his for his troubles. I was unscathed, which is more than can be said for the BMW, one side of which had caved in. This will undoubtedly test Dick Lovett's loyalty to the full.

I retrieved my portable telephone and rang Terry Casey to explain my predicament and apologise for my absence. Then I rang Uncle Waggy, who came to collect me and drove me back to his cottage, where I received my second, and far greater, shock of the morning –

Waggy's wife Linkles had left him a note which said simply that Crouch had been killed in a car crash.

I could not believe it; the message would not sink in. I didn't know what to do, and I can't even remember who I rang to find out what had happened. What with the incident in the car and now this, I must have been in a state of semi-shock.

It transpired that Paul, who had been riding at Newton Abbot, had arranged to meet his girlfriend Tarnya Davies, who had been riding at Uttoxeter, at Colin Brown's Ibex pub at Chaddleworth yesterday evening, after we got home from Devon. They were joined there by Steve Taylor, a great friend of Paul's who writes for the *Sporting Life*. Because Paul and Tarnya had been at different meetings, they both had their own cars. After dinner Tarnya left the pub shortly before Paul, who was in turn followed by Steve. No one knows precisely what happened next, but on the way home Paul's car left the road, hit a tree, and burst into flames. Poor Paul didn't stand a chance as Steve, who tried to get to him, was beaten back by the flames. At home, Tarnya became worried when Paul didn't turn up, and drove back towards Chaddleworth to see what had happened. On the way she passed an ambulance and, on finding Paul's car in flames, assumed that he must have been taken away in it. Tragically, she was wrong.

The rest of the day is a complete haze. My first thoughts were for Tarnya, who had not enjoyed the best of luck this year following the break-up of her marriage to Paul Nicholls. But with Paul Croucher she seemed to be finding happiness again. I thought also of Paul's parents, who I have met on several occasions, and I could imagine their grief, too, as Paul meant so much to them both.

Paul was loved by everyone. He had no enemies, only friends and, after a dreadful series of injuries, he had just enjoyed his best season ever with 51 winners. I'm told that the yards in Lambourn were virtually silent this morning: the village was devastated. Even those who didn't know him personally were shocked, as he had lived in Lambourn since he arrived from Devon to work for Nicky Henderson. Paul's death is a tragic waste of the life of one of the nicest people you could ever wish to meet. God bless him.

Saturday 13 August

Paul's death has overshadowed all other events, but nevertheless I was disgusted to see what had been written in the *Sun* newspaper about my innocuous accident. The headline read: 'Jockey Gee smashes up her car to beat death!'. The article went on to say how I was thanking my lucky stars after making a split-second decision that saved my life. Turning to the subject of Paul's death, the newspaper claimed that Paul had offered me a lift back from Newton Abbot, but that I had turned it down.

It was horrible to read such lies on an awful day like today. I had, in fact, come back from Devon with Paul, and I had certainly not spoken to the *Sun* about his death, or indeed about my own accident.

Sunday 14 August

There was another celebrity gymkhana today, held at the Princess Royal's home, Gatcombe Park. The National Hunt jockeys were represented by Peter Scudamore, Simon Sherwood, Woody and Carl, who was substituting for Brendan Powell. The action was 'predictably unpredictable', to use a footballing phrase, with jockeys disappearing in all directions. Scu brought his lovely family along for the day – his wife Marilyn and sons Thomas and Michael. It was Tom Scudamore who made even the beaten jockeys roll around with laughter on Grand National day. Scu had been leading the race on Strands of Gold when he took a crashing fall at Becher's second time round. After the race Tom came rushing up to his father in the weighing room and said: 'Daddy, were you holding on to the horse's mane?' Scu said that he wasn't, so Tom replied: 'Well, you should have been'!

After Friday's tragic events it was good to get out, and in the afternoon jockey Dermot Browne married his long-time girlfriend, Carol Dawson. Paul was a great friend of Dermot's and, although the celebrations went ahead in true Browne fashion, the occasion was tinged with sadness. There were hundreds of people at the evening party, but everyone's thoughts were still with Paul.

Tuesday 16 August

Dick Lovett has been very good about my accident and has kindly given me a Peugeot 205 GTI to use while the BMW undergoes extensive surgery. Fluffy and I used it to travel up to Middleham in Yorkshire to stay with Dad for a few days.

When Dad first started in racing he was Neville Crump's assistant trainer, and he still obviously loves Yorkshire. I hope he's going to be happy in his new surroundings: he's been working very hard at his new yard, which is picturesque and looks in good condition. Time almost stands still during the summer at Middleham and, when we arrived, we rode out for hours around deserted woods and lanes, which was blissfully peaceful. Fluffy had brought his dogs Paint and Jess with us and they were in their element when we went for an evening walk, as there is a rather high concentration of rabbits in Yorkshire.

Wednesday 17 August

Today was inevitably dominated by Captain Crump, the veteran Yorkshire trainer, whom Fluffy had to interview, along with George Moore, another leading Northern trainer, for an article on training in Yorkshire. Now that Dad is based at Middleham, his son is doing all he can to promote the area as the best place on earth to train racehorses. Judging from what I've seen so far, this is more or less true.

Captain Crump was as brash as ever. He and his wife had just returned from their summer holiday in Majorca. They have been there every year for the past 35 years for three reasons: they enjoy the sun, the hotel staff know their likes and dislikes and a bottle of gin costs £1.50. The poor captain had obviously over-indulged in the cheap alcohol, because when I asked him how he was he replied: 'I've got the runs and I'm too weak to pick my own f. . .ing nose', but apart from that he was in great form. Unfortunately he was of no use whatsoever for Fluffy's article because he talked about every subject under the sun except racing. However, Fluffy was later given some good material by George Moore, who seemed very positive – it is easy to see why he is one of the North's most successful trainers.

Thursday 18 August

Fluffy and I said farewell to Dad and set off back to Berkshire. I volunteered to drive and, as usual, my brother immediately fell fast asleep and remained that way for most of the five-hour journey.

Friday 19 August

Today was Paul's funeral. My mood was not improved by a letter from someone in Taunton, which alluded to the obnoxious rubbish printed in the *Sun* the day after the accident. The letter read: 'Dear Miss Armytage, I should have thought that even you with your notorious resorts to cheap gimmicks could have refrained from tarnishing Paul Croucher's memory by encouraging the *Sun* to print smuttish innuendoes re your "turning him down" etc. Paul Croucher was a gentleman whose memory was not best served by your ceaseless thirst for cheap publicity'. The writer printed his name and address, but I shall not be replying. It was a letter I could have done without.

The funeral took place in Devon, where Paul was brought up, and all his friends travelled down for the service. There were over 300 mourners, which showed just how popular a man he was. It was a terribly sad occasion and, when the coffin was brought into the church with Paul's crash helmet and whip on top, I could not help but cry. There were many beautiful floral tributes, including a wreath from Tarnya accompanied by a note expressing her love for Paul and the happiness he had brought her.

It is hard to remember Paul ever being unhappy, so we all made an effort to remain cheerful. The church walls were lined with statues of angels, and I tried to pick out which one he would be chatting up first. Paul was laid to rest in the churchyard which had a breathtaking view over the Devon countryside that he had ridden over as a young boy.

Everyone seemed drained at the end of the service and quietly drifted away to go home. I had travelled down with Martin, Sarah and Mark Low, a friend of Paul's who used to ride as an amateur. We travelled in Mark's very smart Jaguar automatic, but our journey nearly ended in disaster.

Martin was driving fast along the outside lane of the M4, which was crowded with holiday traffic, when he suddenly announced that the accelerator had jammed and he couldn't free it. As the car was an automatic, our only options were to put it in reverse, which would surely result in an accident, or to cut across three lanes of traffic to the relative safety of the hard shoulder. Martin took the latter option, and unbelievably managed to avoid contact with any other cars before he regained control.

Tarnya, who is coping well, had asked a few friends for a drink that evening at the house where she and Paul used to live. We were only too pleased to go if it helped her, but I was a little anxious about the occasion. In fact, the evening went well and, although Tarnya must have been feeling awful, I admired the way she put on a brave face.

Finally, at the end of this very sad day, I had to crown the Lambourn Carnival Queen. It was not something I would have chosen to do on this particular day, but the winner looked thrilled, and I tried to look happy for the photographs.

Saturday 20 August

This morning's *Sporting Life* had yet more bad news for the racing world: Lester Piggott's wife Susan has been seriously injured on the Newmarket gallops and is now on a life-support machine at Addenbrooke's Hospital in Cambridge. Piggott is the most famous name in racing but the family is currently suffering terrible misfortune.

There were two very touching letters in the *Life* about Paul. One was from Tarnya's parents, simply expressing their fondness of Paul and thanking him for making their daughter so happy. The other summed up just how much Paul had meant to the local community. The letter explained how Paul had remained the same person throughout his years at Lambourn. It said that although he was one of the leading jockeys at the time of his death, he always mucked out in the yard and remained 'one of the lads'. When he had been riding out he always made sure that his horse was done up perfectly, thus making the lads' work that much easier at evening stables. It was a very touching letter signed, simply, 'A stable lad from Lambourn'.

Once again I did not have a ride this afternoon, which meant more frustration and no income. However, in the evening I went to a ball at Stowe School with Carl, Martin, Sarah, Jamie and Bism. For once though, the Saturday night team was off form: Carl and Martin were suffering from upset stomachs. We drove home in the early hours with the male passengers making some rather strange noises.

Sunday 21 August

Carl did not have a very comfortable night, but at least he could look forward to a lie-in as he wasn't due to ride out in the morning. Unfortunately this was not to be, however, as someone came knocking at the front door and wouldn't go away. Carl went downstairs and was confronted by a Jehovah's Witness. Now Carl is most polite, but he is not religious and so he was not best pleased at having his Sunday morning sleep interrupted. His behaviour was not as gracious as it usually is, and I doubt if that particular Jehovah's Witness will call again.

Later in the morning we went to David Nicholson's open day at his yard in Condicote, near Stow-on-the-Wold. It is always a successful day and raises a great deal of money for charity. There were three or four jockeys there and we did our bit by signing autographs at 50p each – a rip-off, but for a good cause!

Monday 22 August

A memorial service for Paul was held in Lambourn this afternoon, enabling many people who had not been able to attend his funeral to pay their respects. The local community turned out in force – jockeys, stable lads and press. Kim Bailey and David Murray-Smith, Paul's two principal trainers, read the lessons and Steve Taylor gave the address, doing so in the true Crouch spirit. Having briefly outlined Paul's career from his first days with Nicky Henderson to his last successful season, he then told an amusing anecdote which until now had been kept secret.

On Gold Cup day at Cheltenham this year Paul was due to ride Aquilifer for David Murray-Smith in the Ritz Club National Hunt Steeplechase. The horse, which had improved out of all recognition during the season, was well-fancied, and David told Paul to walk the course before racing. However, Paul had arrived at the course wearing an expensive new pair of shoes and, as he started to walk round, he found it was very wet. So, bearing in mind his new shoes and the fact that he had ridden at the meeting on the two previous days, he decided to skip his walk and returned to the weighing room for a nap.

In the paddock before the race Murray-Smith, under the impression that Paul had walked the entire course, told him that under no circumstances was he to take the lead until he had jumped the last. As the runners turned into the home straight it was obvious that Aquilifer had every chance of winning, and Paul went to the front as they jumped what he thought was the last. On looking up, however, Paul saw to his surprise that there was still one more fence to be jumped, which they negotiated successfully, striding on up the hill to a famous victory. Paul had forgotten that on the first two days of the Festival meeting the races are run over the old course, while the new course is used on the third day to provide fresh ground for the Gold Cup. The two courses run parallel to one another, but the layout of the fences is slightly different. Paul was always a cool customer, in the nicest possible way, so when he came back to unsaddle the horse he explained to Murray-Smith that Aquilifer wanted to hit the front two out and he didn't want to disappoint him!

After the service most people went to the Swan at Shefford, one of Paul's favourite pubs. It happened to be the first day that pubs in Britain were allowed to stay open all afternoon and, as someone remarked, 'I should think Paul's delighted he was remembered on the first day of all-day drinking!'.

Wednesday 24 August

I rode Highbold for Mrs Cuthbert at Devon and Exeter today. After his poor run at Uttoxeter a fortnight ago, I was told to try to settle him in the early stages and not to let him run away with me – easier said than done. In the event I rather overdid the waiting tactics, dropping him right out behind the rest of the field, but we passed three or four tired horses in the last half-mile to finish fourth. I thought the stewards might have called me in, as I hadn't made much of an effort to put Highbold in the race early on, and I was longing to tell them that I was the only jockey ever to complete the course on this neurotic animal! I do enjoy riding him, though – he is the most brilliant jumper and has a lot of ability as well as character.

In the same race Ronnie Beggan had a bad fall and was taken to hospital with three broken vertebrae. This will rule him out for at least three months, which is not a good way to start the season.

Thursday 25 August

I went to London today to be presented with a trophy by the *Field* magazine for being the leading lady rider for the third successive year. The lunch was held at the Savoy Hotel, and there seemed to be more waiters than guests. They kept piling food on to my plate, so I had no chance of finishing. At the end of the meal I was presented with my prizes – £100 in cash and a gold brooch worth £500, about five times as much as I've earned so far this season.

Saturday 27 August

As this is a Bank Holiday weekend there are plenty of race meetings but, alas, not many rides for me. I was booked to ride Sherpaman for G.P. Kelly in the two-mile selling hurdle at Market Rasen this afternoon, and I travelled up with Fluffy, who had a ride for Jimmy Fitzgerald which stood a very good chance. We gave a lift to Mandy Langton, an amateur who runs a livery yard in Cheltenham and who often rides out for Oliver Sherwood in Lambourn. She was due to ride in the same race as me, and certainly looked to have the better chance.

We set off at 10.00 am, but it wasn't long before we ran into the first of the holiday traffic jams. By 1.30 we were still an hour's drive from Market Rasen, and it was obvious that Mandy and I would miss our rides. We telephoned the course from the car to say that we would be late but that we would arrive in time for Marcus to ride in his race.

We reached the course at 2.35 to find that Mandy's scheduled ride had fallen at the first and mine had finished tailed off, so we hadn't missed much. I met up with Corky and we went down to the last fence to see Fluffy's race, in which his horse started 5–2 on. Unfortunately, Fluffy was beaten into second place by a lady jockey and, to add insult to injury, he admitted dropping his stick at the second last!

In the evening Jamie Osborne held his 21st birthday party at his new house. It was a predictably noisy affair, with most people drinking too much and waking up the neighbours.

Sunday 28 August

I had arranged to play squash at 9.00 am, not a good idea as I hadn't left Jamie's party until the early hours. But I felt much better when I got back from the sports centre to find a message on the answering machine from John Spearing, offering me the ride on Celtic Fleet at Southwell tomorrow. I'm delighted because Celtic Fleet is such a good ride, and even though he is set to carry top weight he is not without a chance.

Consequently, I was in great spirits when I went
to Mum's for lunch. She was entertaining three foreign
riders whom Fluffy was supposed to be looking after.
They are all taking part in the amateur Derby at Epsom
tomorrow as part of the Fengentri series – the British
representative is Mr M. Armytage. To my amazement,
Fluffy turned up at Mum's with yet another woman,
whom he'd met last night at Jamie's party. I don't know
how he gets away with it. One day he's going to find
himself in a mess, with three women turning up on his
doorstep all claiming to be the love of his life.

Monday 29 August

I set off for Southwell in good time today, mindful
of the Bank Holiday traffic problems we had encountered
on Saturday. Celtic Fleet looked very well, having
already run this season. We made all the running, and
his jumping was superb. As we took the sixth last we
were joined in the lead by Cottage Rhythm, which
encouraged Celtic Fleet to quicken up again on landing.
Coming to the next three lengths clear, Celtic Fleet
behaved totally out of character, hardly raising a leg
and galloping straight into the fence. I seemed to roll
forever and when I got up the horse was still motionless.
I feared the worst, but he was soon back on his feet,
having only winded himself. It was a disappointing end
to a promising ride.

Arriving home this evening I heard that Vivian
Kennedy, a promising young conditional jockey with
Fred Winter, had broken his neck in a fall at Huntingdon
and is on a life-support machine in Addenbrooke's
Hospital in Cambridge. Suddenly, my disappointments
today seemed minute in comparison.

Tuesday 30 August

I schooled Highbold first thing, and then telephoned to
find out the latest news about Vivian. It is not good: two
tests have been taken to assess the level of activity in
his brain, and both proved negative. Vivian's girlfriend,
Sarah Betteridge, against whom I used to compete in
showjumping, has not left his bedside and the doctors are
waiting for Vivian's parents to arrive from Ireland. It is
less than a week since Vivian and Sarah became engaged
and, on the morning of the fall, her boss had bought
them a lovely engagement ring as a present as they could
not afford that particular ring themselves.

Wednesday 31 August

Late last night the doctors told Sarah to go home, as
nothing more could be done, and Vivian died with
his parents at his bedside. He was a quiet, unassuming
person who, like Crouch, had a successful career ahead
of him. The only consolation is that he died doing what
he enjoyed best, and what he was best at. This has been a
tragic month for jump racing. There were times when I
thought I wasn't having any luck, but when I think about
the deaths of Crouch and Vivian, and Ronnie Beggan's
bad back injury, I realise that I have very little to grumble
about.

The old adage 'the show must go on' applies to
racing as much as it does to any other form of sport or
entertainment. Every jump jockey accepts the fact that
falling – and sometimes being hurt – is all part of the job.
When you start worrying about falling, or getting very
nervous before each race, the time has come to pack up.

That is not to say that I take a totally laid back attitude
to my riding, although, funnily enough, I was totally
relaxed before the Grand National, and felt no pressure
at all. Your feelings prior to a race depend to a certain

extent upon what sort of horse you are riding, and what sort of chance it has, although I never get very wound up because that makes no difference. Naturally, you get more of a pre-race buzz if your horse is in with a good chance, and it's much more disappointing to lose on a good one than on a no-hoper.

September

Thursday 1 September

August is always a quiet time for me, but even so I am disappointed not to have ridden a winner during the opening month of the season. I am hoping that things will pick up in September.

My first ride of the month was on an old favourite, Highbold, for Mrs Cuthbert at Worcester today. My race plan was to jump out of the gate last but in contention, settle him down and then gradually make up ground from a little before halfway down the back straight, leaving something in reserve for the finish. While Highbold has always shown plenty of ability, he sometimes runs far too free early on and burns himself out.

However, today's plan was not successful. I managed to settle him easily enough, but he made an uncharacteristic bad jump at the second flight and became detached from the field. We dropped further and further behind and eventually finished second last. I'm sure that Highbold will surprise everyone and win a race one day, but I certainly wouldn't want to own the horse that finished behind us today.

I travelled to the course with Hywel Davies and we left as soon as possible to avoid the rush-hour traffic, as the racecourse is very close to the centre of Worcester.

Hywel is great company in the car and can talk at length on any given subject. I have known 'H' ever since he used to muck out for Dad during the school holidays, when his big brother Taffy was first jockey at the yard and Taffy's wife was my nanny. Eventually Hywel became first jockey to Dad, and he has often said how much his two years at East Ilsley helped his career. He has always been a good friend and he has given me very helpful advice about riding, schooling and so on.

Friday 2 September

I rode out Bold in Combat at Terry Casey's this morning in the company of Woody, who was schooling Fred the Tread. Fred the Tread has never run over fences, but he still out-jumped my more experienced horse, who is often none too fluent off the racecourse.

Back at home I waded through a pile of correspondence and spoke to a few trainers about possible future rides.

Saturday 3 September

The first Saturday in September is always the date for the opening meeting of the season at Stratford. The executive there inevitably manages to produce good ground, which means that the meeting attracts plenty of runners, and today was no exception – good ground, big fields, but sadly there were no rides for me. The Scudamore/Pipe combination was successful once again, and Woody produced another brilliant piece of riding to win the two-mile handicap chase on Iron Gray for his guv'nor, David Nicholson.

We spent Saturday night at the Pound, and Fluffy was among the group. As I have mentioned earlier, he greatly enjoys mixing with the opposite sex, but his eagerness to impress his string of girlfriends can sometimes lead to embarrassing situations, and tonight was one of those occasions. On one of his European racing weekends Fluffy had met a stunning Swedish girl called Madeleine with, as he put it, 'legs up to her armpits and a body to match' – the sort of girl we all envy. On his return from Sweden, Fluffy boasted about this beautiful blonde who had fallen in love with him, and who would be coming to stay with him later in the summer. No one believed him until he appeared one evening with Madeleine wrapped round him and announced that she would be staying with him for two weeks. Carl and Luke and the rest of the men were like flies round a cowpat, and Fluffy was revelling in all the adulation. He was also feeling rather pleased with himself that Madeleine's visit coincided with his English girlfriend's holiday.

Tonight, however, Annie returned and 'the lads' decided to do their best to spoil the reunion. They were puzzled when Annie appeared to ignore all their comments about what Fluffy had been up to in her absence, but she was just biding her time. On arriving home, well under the influence, Fluffy slumped on the sofa. Annie crept in from the kitchen with a bowl of water which she poured all over him, the sofa and the floor, before turning tail and departing!

Sunday 4 September

I left home at 7.00 am today to ride out for Terry Casey. It's curious that on my so-called day off I should have ridden out two lots in the morning and numerous other horses at the Kingsclere Hunter Trials in the afternoon. If I could ride as many horses on the racecourse next week I could start calling myself a jockey again.

During the trials I met up with several old school-friends and, as usual, we went down memory lane. I never did much serious studying at school, and my favourite lesson was PE, which I really enjoyed. I used to do stupid things, such as jumping fully-clothed into the swimming pool in the middle of winter for a bet.

September

One end-of-term report read: 'Gaye has many assets,
but it is a pity she doesn't harness more of her energy
into her work, rather than her play'. I was, however,
once given the 'Most Cheerful Pupil' award. I managed
to get a few O-Levels, although Fluffy was the family
swot. My main achievement at St Gabriels was gaining
the record number of order marks in one term. These
were dished out for bad behaviour, and if you were given
only two or three in a term you had some explaining to
do. My personal best was 18, which was announced at
end-of-term assembly amid a disapproving silence.

Tuesday 6 September

Still no rides, so I had to make do with a schooling
session at Terry Casey's. My frustrations were eased
a little this afternoon when I thrashed Carl at squash
without even breaking sweat. Carl was furious, and went
off with Luke for a 'lads' night out' at the funfair
in Wantage. I suspect that their main objective was to try
to tempt half the female population of Oxfordshire back
to their house for coffee and goodness knows what else.
I am convinced that Mr Harvey will be the end of my
relationship with Carl!

Thursday 8 September

I am still riding out regularly for Mr Mitchell. This
has finally brought its reward, as tomorrow I have my
first ride for him as a professional, on Liffey Travel at
Newton Abbot. I badly want to do well on my early rides
for the stable, because if things go well it could lead to
further opportunities, and Liffey Travel is just one of the
many nice horses Mr Mitchell bought in Ireland during
the summer.

   This morning Nigel Coleman and I schooled a total
of 12 horses, and they all jumped well except one – Cross

the Moat, a badly-named horse if ever there was one. This animal was responsible for Ronnie Beggan's serious back injuries last month and is, despite numerous schooling sessions, quite the worst jumper I have ever ridden. Much to my relief, Mr Mitchell has decided against running the horse until it shows that it is a reasonably safe conveyance.

Friday 9 September

Today was another of those days that make you realise what a great leveller racing is. I had hoped to give Liffey Travel an accomplished ride, but various elements conspired against us. On leaving the paddock we had a disagreement about which side of another horse to go and, in the ensuing fracas, I was lucky to escape unscathed as I narrowly avoided being trampled on by two other horses after falling off. Meanwhile, Liffey Travel headed off for an unscheduled circuit of Newton Abbot and I put as much distance as possible between myself and an irate trainer. Liffey Travel and I were reunited at the start, and she seemed none the worse for her pre-race exercise, finishing fifth under what I thought was a sympathetic ride. However, Mr Mitchell did not agree and tore me off a strip, which I deserved, saying that I gave the horse too much to do. I returned home with my tail between my legs and a large bruise on my bottom.

Saturday 10 September

Every licensed jockey in Britain seemed to have a ride today except Luke and me, although Luke at least has a valid excuse in that he broke his collar-bone at Devon and Exeter ten days ago. Some cynics have suggested that he would probably ride better in this condition, but Luke is not bothered by these remarks and is planning to spend some of the weekend drowning his sorrows.

September

Today was my 23rd birthday. Carl forgot (he says he never knew), but we went out for a meal in the evening with some of the usual crowd and had a good night.

Sunday 11 September

One of the highlights of the Racing Calendar took place today – the Lambourn Superstars event. It was organised by Mark and Sarah Bradstock in aid of the Carlo Parry Fund. Carlo, who used to ride for Nick Gaselee, tragically died of cancer a few years ago and his friends decided they would hold an annual event in his memory to raise money for cancer research. There was football, BMX bike racing, an obstacle race and a wheelybin relay race.

I was in the celebrity team, along with such luminaries as John Francome and Brough Scott, but Captain Forster's team were installed as ante-post favourites for one very simple reason: Luke Harvey had failed a fitness test on his damaged arm the previous evening (he was unable to lift eight pints of lager!), and was replaced by a much more athletic person in the shape of his younger brother Giles. This team duly won the competition, but Giles was so exhausted that he fell asleep on the train taking him home to Tiverton and ended up in Exeter. It was a great day and another success for a very worthy cause, raising over £10,000. As usual, Carlo's parents travelled from their home in Wales to present the winning team with their trophy.

Monday 12 September

Another glamorous day in the life of a struggling jump jockey.

I had one booked ride at Southwell, Sherpaman for G.P. Kelly, for whom I often ride when I venture North.

Unfortunately, it had no realistic chance of winning and we finished last. As Southwell is about 80 miles from Dad's new yard at Middleham, I decided to stay with him for the night. I would undoubtedly have got lost had I tried to drive myself there, so I hitched a lift to Southwell with Jamie Osborne, and travelled on to Middleham with Paul Harte, a conditional jockey based there. Dad was pleased to see me and sounded optimistic about his new training venture.

Tuesday 13 September

Dad is one of the old-fashioned breed who believe that staying in bed after 5.00 am is unhealthy and a waste of time, so, even though the Middleham gallops do not open until 7.00 am, he is always up at 4.45 to organise his string. Neither of his children has inherited this habit of getting up in the middle of the night, but this morning we pulled out at 6.30 and, needless to say, we were the first on the gallops.

Dad's new yard is still not fully operational, so we spent the rest of the day fixing doors and windows and rearranging feed bins. After supper I went early to bed, mindful that once again I will be woken at an hour when even the horses are still sleeping.

Wednesday 14 September

After riding out three lots I set off on my train journey from Northallerton to Newbury. It took so long that I vowed never to travel to Yorkshire by train again.

Thursday 15 September

One day Yorkshire, the next Somerset. I drove to Ron Hodges' yard near Somerton this morning to school

Top Gold, who I am booked to ride in the ladies' race at Huntingdon tomorrow.

Nearing my destination I called Brendan on the car-phone. He rides out regularly for Mr Hodges and I wanted to make sure I was going in the right direction. It turned out that Brendan was also riding out for the yard this morning, and was about a mile behind me, so we could have travelled down together! I waited for him in the next lay-by and we drove the final five miles together, a decision I later regretted as I finished schooling an hour before him and had to wait for him.

Friday 16 September

I finished fifth on Top Gold, a small but gutsy horse, but Brendan had a crashing fall from Akram in the two-mile handicap chase. He was concussed and stood down for the mandatory seven days, although when he came round he looked so dishevelled that I thought he might be off for three weeks.

The fall happened at the first fence. When the field came round the second time Brendan was still lying where he fell. The remaining runners were directed away from him by two large orange discs placed in the fence in line with his prostrate body, but even so Brendan was very nearly trodden on by one of the horses. A few weeks ago Chris Grant fell and broke his leg at Market Rasen and, despite the discs, he was hit by another horse on the second circuit. The system is not satisfactory and will have to be changed before someone is seriously injured.

Saturday 17 September

My services are not required at either Bangor or Warwick today and I am beginning to become a bit depressed about the lack of rides. I rode out at Mr Mitchell's, a six-hour round trip which at least took my mind off things.

I didn't even feel like going out tonight, although I normally look forward to Saturday evenings. I did various meaningless tasks around the house, cooked supper and went to bed early, as I have to be up by 6.00 am tomorrow.

Sunday 18 September

I made an early start, setting off for Stratford racecourse to ride out Just Acquitted for Mr Mahon. The horse worked well and I'm looking forward to his first run. On my way home I called in at John Spearing's yard to see my old friend Nodalotte, only to discover that he is still at his owner's farm and won't be back in training for another two weeks.

This afternoon was the annual jockeys' showjumping competition held at Childrey. Matt McCormack, who trains nearby, hosted a lively pre-lunch drinks party at which Luke was in particularly good form. Nevertheless, he still managed to jump the fastest clear round in Stage One of the competition. Jamie Osborne knocked a few fences down, despite some expert tuition from Bism, and Jamie Railton, a conditional jockey attached to Nicky Henderson's yard, somehow contrived to jump the wrong course. The overall winner was Martin Bosley, who gave a faultless display of showjumping. He was delighted with his first winner of the season, and even more delighted to beat Luke. Once again I failed to impress the gallery and I don't suppose anyone now believes that I was a competent showjumper in my younger days.

Monday 19 September

No racing, so I helped Mum in the yard and spent some time trying to secure some rides for later in the week. Jack Berry, who is having his best ever season on the Flat, has booked me to ride Wizard of Wos at Sedgefield tomorrow. The journey to the Teesside track will test my limited powers of navigation to the full, but at least Tarnya Davies has a ride there too, so we can get lost together.

The infamous pairing of Messrs Bosley and Harvey went car-hunting this afternoon, as Luke is bored with his Escort XR3i. Despite annoying all the local garage owners, Luke couldn't find a car that would 'pull the women', but Martin managed to pick up a Montego. Luke is green with envy, for not only does the car have a turbo engine and go-faster stripes, but Martin has also had his name stencilled on both sides of the car. That, along with yesterday's showjumping, brings the score to Bosley 2, Harvey 0.

Tuesday 20 September

Sedgefield is not a very popular course with the jockeys, nor is it very easy to find, as it's in the middle of nowhere. However, the executive is enthusiastic and the crowd is usually pretty good.

For once I felt I had a realistic chance of riding a winner. I was travelling very easily throughout the race, although Wizard of Wos was jumping and hanging violently to the right. After I jumped the last I opted for the outside (right) rail to help guide the horse up the run in but, as soon as I did this, Wizard of Wos started to hang to the left! The result was that we were beaten half a length by a horse ridden by Anthea Farrell, who has taken over the ladies' rides for Nigel Tinkler. I was far from pleased with myself for not keeping my horse straight. Tarnya fared even worse: her mount was unplaced, so the six-hour journey home seemed very long indeed, and it was midnight by the time we were back in Berkshire.

Wednesday 21 September

As I had no ride at Devon and Exeter today, I spent
the afternoon gardening. My garden was looking like
a tropical rain forest, so I hacked down all the weeds,
nettles and thistles and lit a huge bonfire. Unfortunately,
I forgot to take the wind direction into account and the
smoke blew straight into the neighbours' garden, where
the day's washing was hanging out to dry. It became
covered in black soot and no doubt smelled like an
ashtray, so I ran into the house and pretended not to be
in.

Carl had a ride in the selling hurdle at Devon which
had a chance of winning, something he would
appreciate as he's had only one winner this season. I
discovered the result on Ceefax – the horse was unplaced
– so I rang Carl in the car to find out what had happened.
The carphone was answered by Willy MacFarlane, who
explained that he was driving the car home as Carl's
horse had slipped up on the final bend. Carl had been
kicked by the following horse and was in hospital with
concussion and a suspected broken arm.

I rang the hospital to find out about Carl's condition.
I was relieved to hear that he had regained consciousness
and would be able to leave the following morning, so I
arranged to collect him then.

Thursday 22 September

After riding out at Mr Mitchell's I drove to the hospital
to collect Carl, who was looking decidedly pale, with his
left arm hanging limply at his side. Concussion means an
automatic seven-day ban from riding but, judging from his
appearance, it will be considerably longer before he rides
again. He slept all the way home and still looked very
drawn and tired when we arrived.

The first thing a jockey does on arriving home is to
head for the answering machine to see how many trainers

want his services. Despite his enforced lay-off, this is
exactly what Carl did. I suppose it was obvious whose
voice would come on first: Luke Harvey's. 'This is the
Devon and Exeter General Hospital, Mr Llewellyn.
We have the results of your tests and have reached the
conclusion that you are a complete wimp and there is
nothing wrong with you at all.' Luke then broke off. I
thought he was going to show some sympathy, but all he
wanted to know was which rides Carl had lined up, and
could he stick him in for some spares? Typical Harvey,
and we had to laugh.

Carl was very stiff and not talking a great deal of sense.
I reckon it will be at least two weeks before he recovers.
I even had to bath him tonight – if this becomes a habit it
should give me some idea about when he is feeling better!

Friday 23 September

After Dad moved up North, Mum planned to build a
new yard in East Ilsley, partly funded by the proceeds of
the sale of Nelson House. However, as each day goes
by the cost of building seems to rise and new problems
keep cropping up. Although Mum would dearly like to
stay in the village, she now accepts that building a new
yard is not viable and is looking to buy an existing
establishment. With this in mind we took four horses
over to Crudwell in Wiltshire this morning to look at
a place which is currently on the market. It turned
out to be a lovely yard, very picturesque, ideally situated
and with plenty of paddocks. Fluffy and I rode work
on the one-mile circular all-weather gallop, which will be
very good after some minor adjustments. Mum was
obviously taken by the place and I think she will make an
offer.

Carl still looked badly shaken when I visited him in
the evening, although bathtime didn't take quite as long
as last night. The only good thing to be said about this
fall (apart from bathtime), is that the Olympics are on.
So while Carl is being entertained, I am subjected to a

constant diet of such fascinating sports as rowing, diving, weightlifting and – the most thrilling of all – smallbore rifle shooting. At least some of the commentators are entertaining as they unwittingly outdo each other in the Colemanballs stakes. The best remark I have heard so far is: 'If he wins the competition, he'll be assured of the gold medal'.

Saturday 24 September

Mum's first runner, You Can Be Sure, was entered for the novice hurdle at Stratford today, which meant I had a ride at last.

There was a rush to get to the course on time because Fluffy insisted on being picked up from his house in Sparsholt rather than meeting us en route. Corky came too, and we all took the micky out of him for scrounging another lift. He was strangely subdued, probably because he's about to leave *Pacemaker* and is wondering if he has made the right decision. He also had to put up with three whippets trying to sit on his head. When Mum asked him if he was comfortable, he smiled politely and pretended to like dogs.

You Can Be Sure ran well to finish sixth and the horse's connections were satisfied. I was hopeful of riding a winner in the ladies' race on Crimson Lady, which started favourite, but we never got into the race, and finished seventh. Penny Ffitch-Heyes won on Point Made, trained by Jenny Pitman, and looked understandably delighted with her efforts for the country's leading lady trainer.

An old friend of mine, Johnny Portman, who now works in France, is here for the weekend, and a large crowd of us had supper at the Pound. Carl insisted that I went, saying he felt perfectly all right, but I went off thinking that if he had a bath tonight I would be more than interested to know who was helping him!

Johnny was in great form. His mother has a horse in training with Mum, called Cardinal's Outburst, which

September

I'm due to ride at Ludlow on Wednesday. As Johnny has ridden him under rules, I quizzed him about riding tactics and he told me he goes best when held up for a late run.

Sunday 25 September

No riding out, no schooling, so I had looked forward to a long lie-in. But, due to lack of exercise, Carl was unable to sleep and was up at a very early hour to watch more fun and games from the 25th Olympiad. I couldn't bear any more of it so I attacked the garden, an occupation they'll probably have in the next Olympics, as every other known form of outdoor activity seems to be taking place in Seoul.

Wednesday 28 September

Cardinal's Outburst started a 33–1 outsider at Ludlow today and won unchallenged by ten lengths. So much for riding instructions.

Both Mum and Mrs Portman echoed Johnny's views that the horse runs best when held up and said that that was how I should ride him today. However, he has been known to refuse to start so, as we came out of the gate, I gave him a couple of backhanders to remind him what his job was. This certainly did the trick, because he simply took off with me and made every yard of the running. Mum has trained a winner from only her second runner and I've actually ridden a winner at last. A good day's work all round.

Martin Bosley would probably not agree, however. He drove Woody to Ludlow in his new sponsored car and, no doubt encouraged by his passenger, put his foot down on the M5 to give the car its first serious 'blow-out'. Within minutes he was flagged down by an unmarked police car, which had recorded him travelling at 107 mph. The result will be a hefty fine and a month's driving ban. If that wasn't bad enough, he was completely run away with in the novice hurdle and finished last.

Friday 30 September

As I wasn't involved with racing today I spent the time looking for a new home for my pet duck Dickinza, who has to leave her present base as the yard will soon be taken over by builders. After much deliberation I decided that her new home will be with an eccentric old lady who lives on the downs with a menagerie of dogs, cats and ducks. I went up there to have a look at the place and was greeted by a very angry-looking Alsatian who, according to the old lady, 'keeps the foxes away'. At the time, however, it was pinning one of the ducks to the ground! On the other hand, the ducks have access to a swimming pool, and at night they sleep in a hay barn for protection.

Dickinza has been the target of many jokes over the past two years, but I shall miss her – I just cannot help my soft spot for any animal or bird in need of help.

October

Sunday 2 October

No peace for the wicked. I had to travel to Stratford
to ride Just Acquitted a piece of work for Jim Mahon.
He insists that whoever rides him in his races rides him
some work at home, too. I had to be there by 8.00 am,
which meant a 6.00 am start. Still, Woody has to do this
sort of thing every Sunday whereas I need to do it only
occasionally.

Pete, my new lodger, moved in today. He is a chef at
the Swan pub in the village and seems pretty easy-going,
so I expect it will work out. I can't afford to pay the
mortgage on my own, so taking in a lodger is essential to
my cash flow.

Monday 3 October

No rides today. Jessica Charles-Jones had a bad fall at
Southwell and has damaged her back. Vertebrae problems
are bad enough, but she apparently couldn't feel her feet,
which sounds very ominous.

Tuesday 4 October

The atmosphere in the weighing room at Devon and
Exeter was very depressing today, an all-too-frequent
occurrence this season. John Buckingham told me that
Jessica will probably never walk again. Jess, never walk
again! It is a sobering thought for any jockey when a
colleague is hurt, but when it is a friend, and hurt so
badly, it is terrible. I could not believe what I'd heard.
One moment she's as fit as a fiddle and riding at her best,
the next she's paralysed for life. We don't yet know the
extent of the paralysis, but I just can't imagine how I
would feel in her situation.

My mind was briefly taken off the subject when
I was legged up on to a horrible little filly. On her
only previous run over hurdles, she fell and broke
Luke Harvey's collar-bone. She is an awkward, contrary
animal who would not even look at the hurdles before
the start, then did not want to line up and had to
be led in. We got as far as the fourth before she refused.
In contrast, Young Nicholas gave me a beautiful ride to
finish second. He's the type I'd like to ride every Monday
to give my confidence a boost for the week. He is trained
by John Roberts, who is always very fair and a great
person to ride for.

Wednesday 5 October

Just Acquitted ran well enough at Cheltenham on ground
harder than he would ideally like, blowing hard but
finishing just out of the placings.

I went to Fluffy's for supper, along with Carl, Tarnya,
Charlie Morlock, Richard Phillips and Martin and Sarah.
Needless to say, I had to take a pudding and, when I got
there, I had to cook the lamb as well! I am due to ride
Celtic Fleet at Cheltenham tomorrow, so I slipped home
early to get to bed at a reasonable hour.

Thursday 6 October

When I arrived home from riding out I discovered I had
been jocked off Celtic Fleet by Scu. It's frustrating, but
I suppose that if the Champion offers his services it's
not something an owner or trainer would turn down. I
went to the course, though, as I had arranged to meet my
carphone sponsors there.

During the second race Jackie Scott, a girl I knew
vaguely from the weighing room, had a bad fall,
smashing her wrist. There is a rule that a racecourse
must have two ambulances on hand for each race, so if
someone whose life is not in immediate danger needs
hospital treatment, another ambulance is sent for. This
can take ages, so I offered to take her instead. She was
in a certain amount of pain, although she was being
very brave – goodness knows what I'd have done if
she'd passed out on the way! I arrived back at the course
worried that I'd missed my sponsors, but it transpired
that they had not been able to make it anyway.

What a day! However, any problems that Jackie or I
had were put firmly into perspective this evening when I
rang Jessica. She is quite amazing – so chirpy you'd think
she was on holiday somewhere. The doctors hope that
she will regain the use of her neck and waist, but they
are adamant that she will be paralysed from the waist
down for life. Despite this, she says she is determined to
be walking again in a year or two, and she certainly has
the right attitude. Her courage and cheerfulness are an
example to us all.

Friday 7 October

I had my first ride for Terry Casey today on a horse
called Laurie's Panther. At last my trips to ride out
for Mr Casey are starting to pay dividends. The
horse ran well to finish sixth and he should improve

on that. He's been off the course for three years
with bad legs but was once a useful performer on the
Flat.

Saturday 8 October

I rode out for Mum at Compton this morning, but
although there are twice as many meetings on a Saturday,
and therefore, in theory, twice as many rides, none
of them came my way. No rides on a Saturday is a
disaster.

Luke had the same problem and was feeling suicidal.
In the evening he and Carl went to the wedding reception
of one of Captain Forster's lads but I decided to give it a
miss and went instead to the Pound at Goosey with some
of the usual gang.

Monday 10 October

A quiet day and, the way things are going, it won't be
the only one I'll have this winter. So I took the chance to
spend the afternoon getting to grips with my accounts
and expenses, and catching up with my correspondence.
Among my recent correspondents there have been people
who want to marry me; young boys who want to get
into racing; and a handful of pensioners.

Jessica has been moved to a specialist spinal hospital at
Odstock near Salisbury. She's got her husband Gareth's
mobile 'phone by her bed, so I rang her again this
evening.

Tuesday 11 October

The ground is still extremely firm, as I found out when
I landed painfully on it this morning. A young horse I

was riding out bucked and whipped round on landing: I sat out the buck but went out the side door on phase two. I managed to hold on and hop back on, but not before the incident was witnessed not only by all Mum's lads but also by Kim Bailey's string! I suspect this episode might take a bit of living down.

Thursday 13 October

I rode Young Nicholas at Wincanton. He started favourite, and I think the connections had backed him because they were disappointed when he finished only fifth. This was because the race was not run to suit him and he didn't jump at all well, something that happens with many horses when they are going faster than their cruising speed. I suggested running him over a longer distance before reverting to chasing – I gather that he is not the best over fences, in fact Luke told me he is desperate.

I also rode Came Cottage for Mr Mitchell. The horse finished third and will make a nice chaser one day, but Mr Mitchell was not happy, saying I went too wide. 'I thought you were going to join me in the stands', was the gist of his remarks. To be honest, and we both agreed on this, I did go too wide but it did not actually cost me the race.

In the evening I watched the Desert Orchid of showjumping, Next Milton, on television. He is wonderful to watch, and to ride too I would think, and tonight he won yet again. I still follow showjumping quite closely, having set my heart on being a top showjumper in my schooldays. However, circumstances diverted me into racing: among them the immense cost of showjumping without a sponsor, a brute of a horse called Bucks Green who forever let me down, and the fact that my third ride in public was a winner.

Saturday 15 October

This evening Mr and Mrs Dunwoody Senior invited
the usual team to dinner to celebrate Woody's sister
Gail's 21st birthday before she disappears for two weeks'
holiday in the sun. Unfortunately, several guests arrived
looking rather bedraggled. Mark Low's receding hairline
was retreating faster than the tide at Morecambe; Chris
Nash had been on the combine for 14 hours; Martin had
been wasting; Corky was late and therefore embarrassed;
and Woody had had yet another crashing fall that left
his face a display of assorted colours and very swollen.
On top of all this, poor Gail herself had a mild attack of
'flu.

However, none of this prevented the men eating the
Dunwoodys out of house and home and drinking all
their champagne, nor did it prevent Mark Low assuming
the starring role, as is his custom. This time the topic of
conversation was his erratic driving. Lowy is not a shy
man and was once spotted driving through Newmarket
at 4.00 am dressed in a mini-skirt, suspenders, a T-shirt
with two balloons stuffed inside, a blonde wig and layers
of lipstick. Fortunately, he had not been drinking, but
the policeman who stopped him was not impressed when
Mark kissed him goodnight!

Tuesday 18 October

No rides today. I have been experiencing some pain in
my back – nothing serious but enough to cause some
discomfort – so I went to see a specialist, Neil Swan, who
treats several racing drivers for G-force injuries. He told
me that the cause was probably playing squash: I must
admit that I do rather over-exert myself on the court,
throwing myself in all directions in an effort to keep up
with the opposition.

Thursday 20 October

An eventful but unsuccessful day. For the 522nd day
running I had arranged for someone to give me a lift to
the races, but disaster struck at 8.30 am.

My drivers for the day, Hywel Davies and Graham
McCourt, could not be contacted anywhere, and I
eventually discovered that they had left for Uttoxeter
without me. Despite several frantic 'phone calls, I was
unable to find anyone else going there, so at 9.15 I set off
alone, hoping that the little sense of direction I possess
would not let me down. However, salvation came 15
minutes later when I received a call on the carphone from
Jamie Osborne. He was only a couple of miles behind
me, so we met up at the next service station, and went
on together in his car. There is no licensed jockey riding
in Britain who drives to the races less often than I do – a
record to be proud of!

On arriving at the lady jockeys' changing room, I
discovered that there was no loo paper, so I went to
the men's changing room and asked Tom Buckingham
for a roll. I should have known better. A minute later
Tom appeared at the door with armfuls of Andrex,
accompanied by 20 jockeys all singing loudly 'We know
where you're going! We know where you're going!' The
trouble was, after that, I couldn't!

The result of the race was disappointing: Young
Nicholas, whose connections fancied him strongly, could
finish only sixth, unable to stay three miles or to act on
the heavy ground. However, not one jockey swore at me
during the race, which must have meant that either I rode
quite brilliantly or they've given up trying to teach me to
ride. I like to think it's the former. . .

Charlie Brooks, who has now taken over the training
licence from Fred Winter, and Woody joined us for the drive
home. Charlie had several outrageous suggestions for
subjects that should be covered in this book. One idea
was that I should talk about all my previous boyfriends
(who don't exist) and explain how they all left me after

only a month, complaining of exhaustion and the weals I used to leave on them (definitely not true!).

Friday 21 October

It was very foggy when I rode out first lot at Terry Casey's yard this morning. I returned home to prepare for the Newbury races, where I had a ride on Pollen Bee, although it was more of a confidence run than anything else. A hug and a kiss from Scu afterwards made up for his yelling at me as we rounded the final turn: he just needed a bit of light and admitted I was doing nothing wrong. That apart, no one has sworn at me for two consecutive races now!

Fluffy had a winner on Major Match at Ludlow today and Carl won on Pegwell Bay for Captain Forster. He even managed to find his way over to my place for supper later on.

Rumour has it that I shall be riding Gee-A in the Mackeson Gold Cup next month. Rumour also has it that woe betide me if he doesn't run well. . .

Saturday 22 October

National Hunt jockeys gathered for their weekly food and drink session this evening. When it comes to paying the bill on these occasions, Carl and I tend to take it in turns on alternate weeks. However, if I plan things right, I get to pay at McDonald's while he takes care of the more extravagant evenings out! I don't think that paying for his girlfriend rates very highly in his list of priorities.

Carl and Luke were both amazingly well-behaved, but I managed to knock over two glasses of wine and spray sweetcorn all over the table, earning myself a 'don't do that again' look from Carl.

For some reason though, everyone seemed rather deflated tonight and drifted off home at an early hour.

Sunday 23 October

I had a squash court booked in Wantage at 9.00 am and, as no one else is prepared to get up at 8.30 on a Sunday morning, I dragged Carl out of bed, much to his annoyance. By the time we had finished playing, and I had won 6–0, he was even more infuriated and threatened not to buy me lunch.

However, we did in the end have a very good lunch at the Mermaid in Burford, guaranteed to undo all the good work accomplished on the squash court. After eating far too much we descended on the Dunwoodys; but although a video had been hired, everyone was fast asleep in front of the fire by the time the credits rolled. The batteries are now sufficiently charged for the coming week.

Monday 24 October

I rode out at Peter Jones' yard near Marlborough this morning. The owners of Rambling Echo want a girl to try to persuade him to jump with a bit more zest. During schooling he was windy and cautious and also very hesitant until about the fourth time up, but I'm looking forward to giving him a spin round Wincanton on Thursday.

Thursday 27 October

At my suggestion I schooled Rambling Echo again this morning, in preparation for his run this afternoon – it may help to remind him what he's supposed to do in the race. It was bucketing down with rain and I got soaked, but the horse jumped better than last time.

It had stopped raining by the time I arrived at Wincanton, where I was also riding Roving Glen in Division One of the novice chase. We went a very fast gallop most of the way – some critics might have said too fast early on – but I was upsides Scu and I thought he ought to know as much as anyone about pace. In the end Woody, who had been sitting quietly behind until the last, came through to beat us both. I was third, but I'm sure Roving Glen will win a race soon. It would be lovely if all horses jumped like him.

In Division Two Rambling Echo jumped almost as well, much to my surprise, and ran very well until the pressure was on and he was actually asked a question. Once that happened he very soon called it a day, and we were eventually tailed off.

Friday 28 October

I went to Devon and Exeter today feeling confident that I would ride a winner. At last the ground was soft enough for Celtic Fleet and everything seemed to be in his favour. How wrong I was – we pulled up two out. He was exhausted; Mr Spearing's horses are always very fit so there is obviously something not quite right with him.

I travelled home with Messrs Dunwoody, Harvey, Bosley and Llewellyn. We stopped for a game of darts on the way and although I can't say that I won any prizes, I did at least manage to hit the board on several occasions.

Saturday 29 October

I went to Ascot to ride Mr Finlee, an ex-pointer who can't quite manage three miles. Today's run was simply a confidence-booster in a two-mile novice hurdle, and he ran as I expected – we didn't beat many but we achieved what we set out to do.

November

Wednesday 2 November

A day for supporting the rest of the Armytage clan. I
had no rides at Newbury this afternoon, but Marcus
was attempting to guide Sunbeam Talbot to victory
in a competitive two-and-a-half-mile chase at our local
course. Sunbeam performed well enough but, despite
a vigorous ride from Fluffy and some ear-shattering
screams of 'Come on 'Cus!' from our travelling head girl,
Ruth, he could manage only fourth.

Thursday 3 November

I gladly accepted the ride on Shipmate for Terry Casey in
a novice chase at Stratford today. The horse proved to be
rather one-paced, beating only one other finisher, but
at least he negotiated the obstacles safely. He should manage
to win a race as his jumping is outstanding.

As occasionally happens, especially in novice chases,
several jockeys suffered crunching falls. This can make
it difficult, particularly for those at the rear of the field,
to avoid trampling on them. I was alarmed to see Carl's
colours on the ground as we jumped the third, and I

was one of three to go straight over the top of him. It looked like a very heavy fall. He eventually returned to the weighing room, bruised and sore, but actually able to ride the winner of the next race. By this evening, though, only one leg was operational and it is clear that he won't be riding for a few days.

It really is amazing what you can get away with while an injury is still 'hot'. I remember an occasion at Warwick when I fell during a novice chase and a horse trod on the inside of my thigh. Strangely enough, my grandmother, who hardly ever goes racing, was standing right by the fence in question. My leg was extremely painful and the ambulance people at first thought that I'd broken it. However, it was still 'hot' so I managed to ride in the next race. As soon as it had cooled down though, I couldn't touch it. My thigh came up like a great red blister and I was off for two weeks. The same thing happened to me at Liverpool in 1987. The day before the Grand National I had a heavy fall in the Topham Trophy, injuring my knee. I went out and won the next race on Gee-A while the injury was still 'hot', but later on I could hardly walk. The next morning I was hobbling around on sticks and was unable to ride The Ellier in the National.

Friday 4 November

Dr Gee Armytage once again took care of the sick and injured. I spent the afternoon ferrying lame jockeys to Swindon for physiotherapy. Carl is already improving, but race-riding is off the agenda for three days.

Saturday 5 November

No rides, no money. Apart from that, I've never been better!

The only solution was to get Martin to organise

a good Saturday night out, so a major team decided to attend a fancy dress party in Witney. The star, or rather the disgrace, of the evening was Mark Low, who went as an aerobics teacher wearing a revealing leotard which let everything hang out. Quite obscene!

The only absentee was Carl, who is insisting that he will be fit for Monday. He stayed at home with a 5lb bag of frozen peas on his leg – three cheers for Captain Birdseye! These are often used by sportsmen as a substitute ice pack to help reduce pain and swelling.

Sunday 6 November

Carl was still lame, so he declined an invitation to compete in the Injured Jockeys' Fund Team Chase at Warwick today, although he did attend as a spectator.

The jockeys' team, Martin Bosley, Jimmy Duggan, Luke Harvey and Peter Hobbs, was simply disastrous. Luke set the pace, fell and managed to bring down Martin and Jimmy, leaving Peter to finish alone. Luke and Martin remounted to complete the course, but Jimmy went straight back to the beer tent.

Carl continues to insist that he will ride at Wolverhampton tomorrow. I accused him of being totally senseless, because his 'comeback' ride is on a fairly moderate novice chaser, but he maintains that his leg is fine and that the horse jumps well anyway. I'm sure I would do the same in the circumstances.

Monday 7 November

The 'phone rang at 5.30 this evening. It was Woody who told me that Carl had broken his arm in the novice chase at Wolverhampton and asked if I would come and pick him up. A few minutes later Martin rang to say that Luke had broken his collar-bone at Plumpton! You do not need three guesses to work out how I will be spending most of the next week: I will be chauffeur, cook and nursemaid to Llewellyn and Harvey, who will live in the bookie's watching the racing on SIS.

Carl was naturally disappointed about breaking his arm as he will miss many rides over the next three weeks, including Pegwell Bay in the Mackeson Gold Cup.

Tuesday 8 November

I drove the invalids to Didcot to watch the SIS, a closed circuit television channel that provides live coverage of most of the day's racing.

I came home to a blank answering machine, which means no rides in the foreseeable future.

Wednesday 9 November

I schooled Gee-A at Mr Hubbard's yard this morning, but my favourite friend showed little enthusiasm, something the trainer could see for himself. The plan is to run him in the Mackeson, but at this stage I cannot hold out much hope of a good result.

In the evening I drove to London (a feat in itself) to attend a promotional function at Austin Reed of Regent Street. They have been providing the British jump jockeys' team with a travelling 'uniform' for some years now, although I'm the only one in the squad with a skirt! Scu, Woody, Hywel, Brendan, Carl, Graham Bradley and Richard Rowe were among the other jockeys there. Each year the Austin Reed 'Jockey of the Year' receives £500 of clothing vouchers. This time Woody was the recipient, which no doubt pleased him immensely. In the meantime, Carol Dunwoody somehow persuaded one of the Austin Reed directors to let me have a ballgown free of charge.

Thursday 10 November

I actually had three rides at Wincanton today so, although none of them won, at least I'm a quarter of the way to paying this month's mortgage.

Cool Ground and More One Way ran promising races, but my final mount, Snowy Pearl, ran deplorably and jumped as though his legs were tied together. He eventually pulled himself up and, instead of walking quietly back to the unsaddling area, headed off the course though a hedge and into the next field. There he planted himself, refusing to budge, until I was on the point of dismounting and walking back. At that point he decided to make a move, and we came back together, although he insisted on going the long way round.

Saturday 12 November

Mackeson Gold Cup day at Cheltenham. Gee-A is a definite runner in the race, while Scu has taken Carl's place on Pegwell Bay.

Gee-A jumped off in front and led for a mile, after which we lost pace rather rapidly. However, he jumped as well as ever, which pleased Mr Hubbard. In the meantime, Pegwell Bay jumped like a stag for Scu and won by 15 lengths! Many jockeys who miss a winning ride through injury, especially in a big race, are very despondent, but Carl took it well. He was also delighted to see Pegwell Bay prove himself to be a chaser of the highest class and hopes to be fit to ride him in the £25,000 A.F. Budge Handicap Chase at Cheltenham in three weeks' time.

It was quite appropriate that Scu should win the feature race, as the Champion Jockey's Ball was held at the racecourse in the evening. For all his brilliance in the saddle, Scu is not yet an accomplished after-dinner speaker. His speech upon receiving his award consisted of four words: 'Thank you very much'. This was

nevertheless received with rapturous applause. I drove
Carl and Martin home – both were in high spirits, to put
it mildly.

Sunday 13 November

After a pleasurable Sunday lie-in I felt totally rested
as we went to lunch at the Dunwoodys'. How
Woody manages to keep his weight down when he
is married to a cook as brilliant as Carol is a complete
mystery.

Normally on these occasions everyone falls asleep in
front of the Sunday afternoon video, but today's feature
was *Phar Lap*, the story of the great Australian racehorse
of the 1930s. By the end there wasn't a dry eye in the
house.

An idle day, but a very enjoyable one.

Monday 14 November

Back to reality, in my case a 5.30 am start, as I was riding
out at John Spearing's yard near Stratford-upon-Avon.
It was still pitch dark when the first lot pulled out. I
schooled Nodalotte, who is due for a run shortly
and appears to be in tremendous form, which is
encouraging.

Second lot I rode a beautiful filly called Little Brig,
owned by a great enthusiast called Mrs Anne Radcliffe. I
hope for her sake that Little Brig possesses the ability
of her illustrious half-brother Earl's Brig, one of the best
hunter chasers of recent years, who was third in the
1985 Gold Cup. Little Brig is aptly named, as she is tiny,
but she works and schools with great enthusiasm and
is obviously very game. So far, leg trouble has prevented
her from running, but she will be on a racecourse
before too long. I hope that I can get the ride when that
happens.

Friday 18 November

I somehow contrived to be beaten on the 3–1 favourite, Northern Flats, in the ladies' race at Nottingham today. Although the horse was a bit one-paced, I can offer no real excuses. Still, even Scu occasionally gets beaten on a favourite!

Saturday 19 November

It has been announced that Corky has been appointed Secretary to the Jockeys' Association. He is obviously thrilled and will do his best for the jockeys: the best of luck to him.

I went to Warwick today to ride Mr Finlee over fences for the first time. The horse jumped well, finishing fourth. My problems began after I'd finished riding.

The showers in the ladies' changing room were not working because the men were using all the hot water. Eventually, some began to filter through, so I stood under the shower and started to wash my hair, unaware that my towel had mysteriously vanished. At this stage the male jockeys turned off the water, so that I was left stranded in a deserted ladies' changing room with no towel, covered in soap! John Buckingham came to the rescue with a towel which covered only the bare essentials. I soon discovered the identity of the thieves when I heard a round of applause from next door.

Sunday 20 November

I have been asked to appear on *Question of Sport* for the second year running, which is good fun. Once again, the BBC provided me with a chauffeur-driven car to Manchester. I was accompanied by Bism and Corky on the trip, which took four hours as the driver flatly refused to exceed 65 mph.

We were given our own dressing room when we arrived at the studios, and shortly afterwards we sat down to lunch. Corky became engrossed in conversation with Fatima Whitbread and the footballer Ally McCoist, while I was seated near the snooker player Stephen Hendry, Steve 'The Boy' Hodge, who plays football for Nottingham Forest, and big Bill Beaumont, my team captain. I missed Emlyn Hughes, who looked after me on and off the screen last year, but he has since defected to ITV's *Sporting Triangles*.

I am not renowned for my sporting knowledge and I soon made a complete fool of myself with one of my answers. David Coleman asked our team which event started in Luxembourg and finished in Paris three weeks later. Not wishing to be left out of things, I suggested yachting. I wish I hadn't. 'How the bloody hell can you get a yacht into Paris?', enquired big Bill. The answer, of course, was cycling, the Tour de France. After that I only answered questions on racing, which I managed to get right, much to everyone's surprise. In the end our team lost by one point.

Monday 21 November

I rode Tania's Dad for Terry Casey in the novice hurdle at Windsor today but, although we made some progress heading to the last, we still finished in mid-division.

I had also looked forward to riding You Can Be Sure for Mum in the mares-only novices' chase. The horse had improved greatly of late and had reached the stage where winning a race was more of a probability than a possibility. At the last moment, however, my darling brother was given the ride, something he found highly amusing.

The smile was soon wiped off his face. After jumping well at the first seven fences, You Can Be Sure crashed through the eighth for no apparent reason and fired Fluffy into the ground. The result was that he broke his collar-bone and the horse fractured her shoulder. She survived, but will never race again. You Can Be Sure proved to be a great patient and did not appear to suffer too much. She will make a good broodmare. Marcus, meanwhile, will be off for three weeks, which will teach him to pinch my rides!

Thursday 24 November

Another winner at long last! Bold King's Hussar won the £7,000 Wessex Handicap Hurdle at Wincanton today. It was an odd race. No one wanted to make the running on the firm ground so the other jockeys suggested at the start that I give them a lead. I thought Bold King's Hussar would need the race and it was quite a hot little handicap anyway. Without sounding totally negative, I had not been too optimistic about our chances. Besides, on seeing the firm ground, Mum had originally decided not to run him – he won twice last season in the heavy – when his owner, Celia Plunkett, turned up. After much discussion it was decided to let him take his chance.

I set off in front, only hacking, and had he been feeling the ground I would have pulled him up. However, after a while I thought I really ought to quicken the pace. Turning for home I was quite expecting to be swamped by the remainder of the field, but they never came, although I could hear them getting closer. So Bold King's Hussar surprised us all by winning what was really quite a decent prize.

Even my male colleagues were complimentary about the performance – with the exception, that is, of Jamie Osborne, who rode the 7–2 second favourite Blanton Reserve. Hussar had been the 20–1 outsider. Jamie had been going pretty well as we approached the second last hurdle and thought he'd cheekily sneak through on the inside. It gave me great pleasure, as he howled for some daylight, to block off that option. No one gets any favours from me in a race! It effectively meant he had to switch to the outside to pass Bold King's Hussar and Santopadre on my immediate outer. Jamie had eventually finished third and was livid. He reckoned that the manoeuvre had cost him the race. Well, it might have done. I suspect that his pride was dented since he had on this occasion been outgunned by the 'fairer sex'.

Friday 25 November

Much to my horror, my 'yachting' blunder on *Question of Sport* has been given major billing in Martin Trew's column in today's *Racing Post*. Since the programme hasn't been screened yet, the only two people who could possibly have leaked the story are Bism and Corky. And, as Bism is not involved in racing, you don't need to be a detective to work out who the culprit is.

Saturday 26 November

I went to Towcester today to ride Just Acquitted for Mr Mahon, but things did not work out precisely as planned. The horse ran reasonably well first time out at Cheltenham this season, and my instructions today were not to make the running. However, he seemed reluctant to line up at the start, so I gave him a couple of taps just to remind him what his job was, and he simply took off with me. He pinged the first hurdle and, although I tried to get him back, he led until he was headed approaching the second last, where he blundered, and we eventually came in eighth.

Mr Mahon was absolutely fuming – I've never seen anyone so angry! – 'You cannot win a race round Towcester by making the running', he said. 'I do agree,' I replied, 'that they weren't my instructions, but I have won a race round here from the front, on Stray Shot'. It was something I regretted saying almost before I said it. It certainly didn't placate him, so all I could do was apologise and hope it hasn't cost me too many rides.

There are times when no matter how hard you try it becomes impossible to carry out the trainer's instructions. Sometimes another jockey's orders will conflict with mine. A slow pace may well find an animal which is pulling strongly at the front when he is meant to be dropped out for a circuit. Likewise, making the running may prove impossible in a fast-run race.

In the meantime, Luke won the novice hurdle on Glen Oak, a 33–1 shot, so there was plenty to celebrate this evening.

Sunday 27 November

I was back at Towcester this morning where Terry Casey was schooling some of his horses and I was due to partner High Aloft. I left home in plenty of time but arrived ten minutes late, having been stuck in heavy traffic heading for a Sunday market somewhere in the vicinity. It made me furious that I couldn't even go anywhere on a Sunday without getting held up in a jam.

I returned to East Ilsley in time for Mum's last Sunday lunch at Nelson House before she moves. Sarah Betteridge, who was Vivian Kennedy's girlfriend, was among the guests, so it was a poignant occasion in more ways than one.

Monday 28 November

A quiet day with no rides. Martin Trew came to interview me for a piece in the *Racing Post*; in the evening Carl, Corky and Bism came to supper.

Tuesday 29 November

I rode John O'Dee for Mr Hubbard at Huntingdon today. The horse went off at 20–1, but ran well in the lead until two out and we eventually finished third. It was an encouraging run, and he is a pleasure to ride.

Wednesday 30 November

Little Brig had her first outing of the season today, in the two-mile novice hurdle at Hereford. She ran a super race, even though we were in mid-division throughout, eventually finishing seventh, but the main thing was that she came back sound, which is a relief after all the leg trouble she has had.

December

Saturday 3 December

I have to report that my only form of competitive riding today took place in the late hours of the evening. Martin, Sarah, Carl and I were among those invited to a 'race night' in Faringdon, where we had to ride wooden horses up and down a specially constructed track in the town hall. I didn't win a race and even managed to get unseated. This just isn't my season.

Sunday 4 December

Rather a sad day, and certainly not a relaxing one.

Mum finally moved out of Nelson House, so I was busy all day helping to move both horses and furniture to her new yard at Crudwell. When the fourth boxload of horses had been despatched, we dashed over there to prepare the stable lads' hostel. Eventually the move was completed and we came back to East Ilsley for the fifth time to dine with Uncle Waggy and Linkles. Everyone was exhausted and sad that Mum was leaving but, at the same time, we were all optimistic about the new venture. Good luck Mum.

Wednesday 7 December

I was fairly optimistic about Nodalotte's chances in
the two-mile handicap chase at Huntingdon today, but
surprisingly he made a bad mistake at the second fence
and we had a crashing fall.

My leg was quite badly bruised and I was limping by
the time I arrived at Austin Reed's Regent Street store
this evening. It was a special open evening for the public
and Austin Reed had asked various personalities along
to draw raffles, present prizes and so on. I am not the
world's most successful sports person at the moment, but
I still get invited to numerous functions, and I'm as keen
as ever to join in all the fun.

There was a prestigious turn-out of jump jockeys,
all looking very smart in their team kit, supplied by
Austin Reed – Scu, Woody, Hywel and Steve Smith
Eccles were all on parade. In addition there were several
members of Surrey County Cricket Club, which is
also sponsored by Austin Reed, as well as the actor Paul
Eddington from *Yes, Prime Minister* and the actress
Liza Goddard. Afterwards we went on to Silks, Richard
Scott's restaurant in St James's.

Friday 9 December

Mum ran Merryett in a Coral hurdle qualifier at Cheltenham this afternoon. The owners stood to win £5,000
if she finished in the first ten but, despite all my
urgings, we could manage only eleventh. However, the
owners are really nice people and no one looked disappointed.

After the racing there was a meeting between the
jockeys and the Jockey Club's Disciplinary Committee
to discuss the rules governing the use of the whip.
This subject has been in the news a great deal lately,

and five jockeys, including Woody, have recently been given two-day suspensions under the present regulations.

This was Corky's first meeting as Secretary of the Jockeys' Association and I could tell he was a little apprehensive beforehand. However, he needn't have been. Thirty-five jockeys attended the meeting. The stewards were most impressed with the viewpoints raised and informed us that there would be changes to the rules. Scu and Paul Cook spoke very well on behalf of the jockeys.

Saturday 10 December

Bold King's Hussar ran in the handicap hurdle at Lingfield today. As he had won here before and has shown good form of late, the Armytage camp was quietly confident. However, he didn't run quite as well as he did when winning at Wincanton last time out, and after being up with the leaders most of the way he weakened three out, eventually finishing fifth.

The racing entourage then travelled on to London for our friend Caroline Heesman's 21st birthday party, which was held in the very grand setting of the Carlton Club in St James's. It was definitely an occasion for dragging out the best frock. After a delicious dinner the disco burst into life. So did Corky, who launched into his Gary Glitter repertoire. We eventually arrived home at 4.30 am.

Monday 12 December

I went to Warwick today to ride Sweet Storm for Terry Casey, but once again the plans went awry. I received strict instructions beforehand to come from off the pace. However, the horse ran too keenly early on. She eventually burst a blood vessel and I pulled her up. I could almost hear Terry Casey shouting at me from the stands.

After the race I received a quiet but very meaningful

dressing-down, so it was a relief to return to the haven of my changing room, wondering why on earth I chose to ride racehorses as a profession. As I was coming out of the shower, wearing nothing but a wry smile, Terry Casey came in to apologise for the severity of his criticism. I think this was the only time he was pleased to see me all day!

To add insult to injury – although I am not surprised – I have lost the ride on Just Acquitted, who made all the running at Towcester a couple of weeks ago when my instructions were to drop him in. However, Mr Mahon has said that I might get the ride back when the horse goes over fences.

Thursday 15 December

No rides; no earnings; no end to my bad luck: nevertheless jump racing had two notable events to celebrate today. The first was Scu's 100th winner of the season. In achieving this he recorded jumping's fastest-ever century, slashing Jonjo O'Neill's previous record by almost two months. At this rate, if he stays sound, Scu will ride 200 winners this season, a feat never before achieved by a National Hunt jockey.

The second was the wedding of Fred Winter's daughter Philippa to Tom Jacomb. The celebrations were enhanced by the fact that Fred himself, who suffered a serious stroke 15 months ago, was well enough to give her away. She had delayed the wedding until he was able to do this, and they both looked very proud. John Francome and Charlie Brooks were the ushers, and afterwards there was a magnificent party at the Winters' house in Lambourn.

Friday 16 December

I had to undergo one of my dreadful broadcasting experiences today, previewing the £20,000 SGB

Handicap Chase at Ascot tomorrow for *Raceline*. I would have been better occupied searching for a spare ride at one of the other meetings. I called on Richard Phillips to help me with the script, as the wording had to be chosen very carefully: a previous Saturday race preview by Graham McCourt and Jimmy Duggan was banned by the Jockey Club, who considered it to be a tipping service.

After hours of picking and choosing I was horrified to learn that *Raceline* had rejected the whole thing and that the Jockey Club would not have allowed it anyway!

Saturday 17 December

Terry Casey has forgiven me enough for Monday's disaster at Warwick to give me the ride on Tania's Dad at Nottingham today. He's a lovely little horse, a chestnut full of character, who has won over five furlongs on the Flat. Much to my relief, I managed to carry out my riding instructions today, although we could finish only in mid-division.

Carl and I decided to leave the socialising to the others this evening: I am riding out tomorrow morning before we go on to Anabel King's house for what is bound to be a lively lunch.

Sunday 18 December

I was right. Anabel does not do things by halves and she invited about 70 people to pre-lunch drinks. None of them seemed keen to leave, so those of us who had been invited to stay for lunch itself did not sit down to our meal until 3.30. Her lunches usually last a minimum of three hours and today was no exception.

December

Monday 19 December

Towcester on testing ground is a stiff challenge for
any horse, and Pollen Bee, who failed to complete the
course on five occasions last season, was entered in the three-
mile novice chase today. Despite atrocious ground he
jumped well, which should help to restore his confidence.

I also teamed up with my 'best mate' Nodalotte. He
has clearly learned his lesson from his fall at Huntingdon
last time out, for today he jumped immaculately, finishing
second to Woody on Waterloo Boy. This was a good performance, as he probably needed the race, having reached
only the second fence at Huntingdon. I'm sure we will have
much more fun with him soon.

Tuesday 20 December

Dad drove down from Middleham today for his monthly
visit. As usual, he arrived at 6.30 in the morning, so as to
miss the traffic. By my calculations, he must leave home
not much later than 3 am – at that time you'd certainly be
lucky to find any traffic!

However, he did not travel with me to Ludlow to watch
me ride Mr Finlee, which was just as well, for the horse
and I parted company at the second last, leaving me with
slight concussion. Woody, who had fallen at the same
fence on the previous circuit, walked back to the weighing
room with me and convinced me that I'd been unseated.
I thought I was guilty, but on seeing the video I was
just glad to be alive – Mr Finlee had turned a somersault and really fired me into the turf. Thanks, Woody!

Wednesday 21 December

This evening Carl and I went to Mark Wilkinson's lads'
Christmas party. It was held in the local pub and was

quite entertaining, although two of the lads, taking full advantage of Mark's generosity, got so legless they had to be removed from the premises and were last seen face down in a flowerbed.

Thursday 22 December

This was the last day's racing before the Christmas break, although it didn't affect me as I had no rides anyway. I rode out this morning and spent the rest of the day finishing off my Christmas shopping, so I am now virtually penniless.

In the evening all the local jockeys gathered at the Challow Country Club for their annual Christmas dance, organised by Lorna Vincent. It was great fun as usual but, being one of the few sober persons left at the end of the evening, I had to ferry several carloads of people home. Another very late night!

Friday 23 December

I received a healthy crop of Christmas cards in the first post this morning, including one from Dick Lovett Garages wishing me luck in 1989. I was therefore somewhat surprised and depressed to receive a letter from Dick Lovett in the second post, which again wished me luck for 1989 but told me that the sponsored BMW deal is to be withdrawn on New Year's Eve. I now have one week to find another car.

Saturday 24 December

Our first team – Woody and Carol, Martin and Sarah, Chris, Fluffy, Carl and me – went out this evening for a bite to eat and the odd crate of wine. Everyone was in good form and we had a super meal before returning to the Dunwoodys' house to sing carols and exchange gifts. Martin gave Sarah some revealing underwear, but I'm afraid that I can't divulge any details of the other presents, although the presents themselves revealed plenty!

Sunday 25 December

A typical family Christmas Day at my grandmother's house in Stow-on-the-Wold. I met up with my cousin Dete, who doesn't follow the family tradition of horses. Maybe we put him off at a young age as I well remember the day when Fluffy and I enticed him on to our pony bareback. We were supposed to be taking him for a ride. We did. While Fluffy let go of the head collar I cracked the pony over the rump and chased him flat out downhill into a cornfield where the two parted company. He has never forgiven me to this day! The mere mention of horses brings him out in hay fever.

I was rather tired from the previous week's hectic activities, and so I was home by 8.00 in the evening in time to watch my favourite programme, *It'll be Alright on the Night*. I think that expression just about sums up my year.

Monday 26 December

There are eight Boxing Day jump meetings today, and I had two booked rides at Wincanton in front of a crowd of 10,000. Earth Spacer finished fourth in the novice hurdle and Bold King's Hussar was fifth in the Coral Golden Hurdle qualifier. However, the biggest cheer of the day came from the bars, where everyone was watching Desert Orchid win his second King George at Kempton on television.

Carl's arm has still not healed sufficiently for him to ride. I invited him to supper this evening but, to my surprise, he said he wanted to cook for me instead. He told me he had spent ages preparing the meal, so I went over to Wantage in great anticipation, only to find him ripping open a Lean Cuisine dish which I had put in his freezer for myself a few weeks ago!

Tuesday 27 December

I have kept the ride on Gee-A, who ran in the curiously named 'Who Framed Roger Rabbit?' Handicap Chase at Kempton today. He gave me a good feel, but a mistake at the last open ditch put paid to any chances we might have had. I suggested to Mr Hubbard that he should run him at his favourite course, Huntingdon, which will restore his confidence.

Thursday 29 December

I had one ride today, Mac's Gold for Mum at Plumpton. He was up with the leaders for quite a time but proved a bit one-paced on the run in and finished third.

A year ago today I won my last race as an amateur, on Silent Echo at Warwick for the Blackmores. That memory will be with me for a very long time; Echo himself is now in happy retirement.

Saturday 31 December

While reflecting on 1988 I suppose my greatest regret is losing the confidence of the Tinklers, who gave me every chance to become a major force in racing. After some rides which didn't go to plan, and which culminated in the fiasco of Darkorjon, I lost my connection with

December

Colin Tinkler's Full Circle group, since when Graham McCourt has been riding most of their horses with great success and I feel some of those winners would have come my way. But sure as Monday follows Sunday I will be fighting to become leading lady rider again next year.

Despite any minor hiccups of my own, my final thoughts for the year rest with Paul Croucher, Vivian Kennedy, Jessica Charles-Jones and their respective families.

Epilogue
January to July
1989

As I finished my diary for 1988 I hoped that with the
turn of the year my luck would turn too, and that more
rides and winners would come my way. Sadly, however,
that has not yet happened. Rides have been thin on the
ground, winners virtually non-existent. I have had to
bite the bullet by taking a part-time job in a local pub.
In spite of the terrific atmosphere and friendliness in the
Crown and Horns, it is not a job I would choose. But the
mortgage has to be paid, so until things improve I will
have to put up with it.

Last spring I rode Gee-A in the Grand National
amid much media attention – this year, by contrast,
I did not have a ride in either the National or at the
Cheltenham Festival. However, I know that few
jockeys achieve this goal, and I count myself fortunate
to have had the opportunity to ride in the National
in 1988. Far from discouraging me, missing out in
1989 has strengthened my determination, not only to
get a ride in 1990, but one that is capable of winning.
As this book went to press I was negotiating with
a potential sponsor, and if this and other plans come

to fruition I will be on the way to achieving my
ambition.

It is impossible to put my finger on any one reason
why the 1988–89 season was so disappointing for me.
The gap left by the lost connections I have already
mentioned has not been filled by any particular trainer.
I don't blame the trainers – anyone who is able to call
upon the services of such talented jockeys as Richard
Dunwoody would be a fool not to. There are some
owners and trainers who simply will not put up a woman
jockey, no matter how capable she may be, although
I am glad to say that there are many who do give us a
chance to prove ourselves. It is not always a woman's
relative lack of strength that dissuades them – often it
is the fear of injuring her. In view of some of the recent
tragedies this is not surprising.

On her final ride of the last day of the 1988–89 season
Diane Clay, who won the ladies' title (which eluded me
for the first time in four years), fell and broke four bones
in her neck and back. We were all devastated to discover
that her injuries were worse than was first thought and
that she will not be able to race-ride again for at least a
year, if ever. Diane has picked herself up to assist in the
running of her father's yard and she and Richard Bevan,
who will ride for her father next season, have become
engaged and plan to marry next June.

Jessica Charles-Jones is now with her parents-in-law
in Gloucestershire but will shortly be moving to a new
house and yard in Letcombe Regis, not far from me,
where she plans to buy and sell horses while her husband,
Gareth, continues riding. She is looking forward to this
fresh challenge which will keep her involved in racing.
We hope that the arrival of a new, lighter wheelchair and
a specially adapted car will help to minimise her practical
problems.

Just after New Year Nodalotte, one of my favourite
horses, was struck badly from behind just as he was
returning to winning form. His hind leg was lacerated
but happily, contrary to our initial fears, he is recovering.

In general, though, 1988–89 was a marvellous season
for National Hunt racing. The brilliant Pipe-Scudamore

combination dominated, smashing all the records. Scu, with 221, became the first jump jockey ever to surpass 200 winners in a season and Martin Pipe was the leading National Hunt trainer with 213. The ever-popular Desert Orchid won the Gold Cup, and following the retirement of Dessie's jockey, Simon Sherwood, Woody will be taking over the reins. Simon has bought the plot of land opposite my house from my father and plans to train there. I am thrilled that he will be moving into the village – I know that he will make a super job of the yard.

Luke Harvey now has a great job as first jockey to Reg Akehurst. None of his attempts to disguise his delight fools anyone. Early in the evening he plays it cool, but as time wears on his laid-back act begins to crumble as he visualises himself among the top ten jockeys, and by the end of the evening, in typical Harvey style, he is thrashing the likes of Scu to become Champion Jockey! Fluffy too has landed a very good job – as Newmarket correspondent for the *Racing Post*. I am delighted for him although it means I don't see much of him these days.

As for me, I am by no means ready to throw in the towel. I have had setbacks but there are many people worse off than I am. I am determined to carry on in one piece and to work as hard as ever to ride winners.